KU-511-114

a collection of essential MEDITERRANEAN recipes

This edition published in 2011

The Boots Company PLC
Nottingham
England
NG2 3AA
www.boots.com

Copyright © Parragon Books Ltd 2010

All rights reserved. No part of this publication may be reproduced, stored in a retrieval system, or transmitted, in any form or by any means, electronic, mechanical, photocopying, recording, or otherwise, without the prior permission of the copyright holder.

ISBN 504-5-09-776965-7

Printed in China

Internal design by Terry Jeavons and Company

Notes for the Reader
This book uses both metric and imperial measurements. Follow the same units of measurement throughout; do not mix metric and imperial. All spoon measurements are level: teaspoons are assumed to be 5 ml, and tablespoons are assumed to be 15 ml. Unless otherwise stated, milk is assumed to be full fat, eggs and individual vegetables are medium, and pepper is freshly ground black pepper.

The times given are an approximate guide only. Preparation times differ according to the techniques used by different people and the cooking times may also vary from those given. Optional ingredients, variations or serving suggestions have not been included in the calculations.

Recipes using raw or very lightly cooked eggs should be avoided by infants, the elderly, pregnant women, convalescents and anyone suffering from an illness. Pregnant and breastfeeding women are advised to avoid eating peanuts and peanut products. Sufferers from nut allergies should be aware that some of the ready-made ingredients used in the recipes in this book may contain nuts. Always check the packaging before use.

Vegetarians should be aware that some of the prepared ingredients used in the recipes in this book may contain animal products. Always check the package before use.

MEDITERRANEAN

introduction

The Mediterranean Sea is part of the Atlantic Ocean and covers a huge area almost completely enclosed by land, with Europe to the north, Africa to the south and Asia to the east. Countries bordering the sea include Spain, France, Italy, Greece, Turkey, Lebanon, Egypt, Tunisia and Morocco.

The many positive health aspects of what has come to be known as 'the Mediterranean diet' have been widely recognized in recent years. The warm, sunny climate and miles of coastal waters enjoyed by the Mediterranean countries provide a diet that is rich in seafood, with only limited amounts of meat and dairy products, and

a stunning range of colourful, nutrition-packed fruits and vegetables. Plenty of olive oil, with its heart-protective properties, completes the picture of a way of eating that promotes an enviably long and healthy life.

The Mediterranean diet is not only healthy, however – it is also absolutely delicious! Although the countries that border this vast sea have many ingredients in common – aubergines, courgettes, tomatoes,

garlic, onions and fresh herbs, as well as pork, lamb, beef, chicken and an incredible variety of seafood – each country has its own characteristic way of transforming these ingredients into wonderful dishes that taste of sunshine. Perhaps the most popular and well-known cuisines are those of Spain, France, Italy and Greece, but most cultures will include versions of the same, very simple, dishes in their repertoire, such as fish, grilled or barbecued with lemon and herbs, or roast lamb with garlic.

Whether your aim is to enjoy the health benefits of the Mediterranean diet or simply to discover more about the fabulous cuisine of this part of the world, remember to use top-quality ingredients, grown locally if possible, and to allow plenty of time to relax over your meal!

soups &
starters

Eating in countries around the Mediterranean is a leisurely, sociable affair, and meals often start with a selection of starters, such as the Spanish tapas or the Greek and Middle Eastern meze, to linger and chat over.

Olives are a simple and very typical way to start – they are served throughout the area, and are perfect with a glass of chilled sherry or white wine, so keep a bottle of Cracked Marinated Olives in the refrigerator to dip into. Chickpeas form the basis for a tasty Tunisian soup, a delicious Hummus dip, and Falafel, crisp little balls flavoured with garlic and spices. Aubergines are used in several countries to make an irresistible dip – Baba Ghanoush is the Middle Eastern speciality.

Fish, as you might expect, makes frequent appearances as a starter. It is often cooked in batter – Calamari, deep-fried squid, is served in most seaside restaurants. Monkfish, Rosemary & Bacon Skewers and White Fish & Caper Croquettes are popular Spanish tapas, and Boreks are filo pastries from Turkey, filled here with tuna and tomato.

Stuffed Vine Leaves are a feature of a Greek meze, while Artichokes with Vièrge Sauce and Asparagus with Hollandaise Sauce are elegant starters, typical of French cuisine.

vegetable & bean soup

ingredients

SERVES 4–6

225 g/8 oz fresh broad beans

2 tbsp olive oil

2 large garlic cloves, crushed

1 large onion, finely chopped

1 celery stick, finely chopped

1 carrot, peeled and chopped

175 g/6 oz firm new potatoes,
    diced

850 ml/1^1/$_2$ pints vegetable
    stock

2 beefsteak tomatoes, peeled,
    deseeded and chopped

salt and pepper

1 large bunch of fresh basil,
    tied with kitchen string

200 g/7 oz courgettes, diced

200 g/7 oz French beans,
    trimmed and chopped

55 g/2 oz dried vermicelli,
    broken into pieces, or
    small pasta shapes

pistou sauce

100 g/3^1/$_2$ oz fresh basil leaves

2 large garlic cloves

1^1/$_2$ tbsp pine kernels

4 tbsp fruity extra virgin
    olive oil

100 g/3^1/$_2$ oz finely grated
    Parmesan cheese

method

1 If the broad beans are very young and tender, use them as they are. If they are older, use a small, sharp knife to slit the grey outer skins, then 'pop' out the green beans.

2 Heat the olive oil in a large heavy-based saucepan over a medium heat. Add the garlic, onion, celery and carrot, and sauté until the onion is soft, but not brown.

3 Add the potatoes, stock and tomatoes, and season with salt and pepper. Bring to the boil, skimming the surface if necessary, then add the basil. Reduce the heat and cover the pan. Simmer for 15 minutes, or until the potatoes are tender.

4 Meanwhile, make the pistou sauce. Whiz the basil, garlic and pine kernels in a food processor or blender until a thick paste forms. Add the extra virgin olive oil and whiz again. Transfer to a bowl and stir in the cheese, then cover and chill until required.

5 When the potatoes are tender, stir the broad beans, courgettes, French beans and vermicelli into the soup and continue to simmer for 10 minutes, or until the vegetables are tender and the pasta is cooked. Taste, and adjust the seasoning if necessary. Remove and discard the bunch of basil.

6 Ladle the soup into bowls and add a spoonful of pistou sauce to each bowl.

bouillabaisse

ingredients

SERVES 4

100 ml/3^1/$_2$ fl oz olive oil

3 garlic cloves, chopped

2 onions, chopped

2 tomatoes, deseeded and
chopped

750 ml/1^1/$_4$ pints fish stock

400 ml/14 fl oz white wine

1 bay leaf

pinch of saffron threads

2 tbsp chopped fresh basil

2 tbsp chopped fresh parsley

200 g/7 oz live mussels

250 g/9 oz snapper or
monkfish fillets

250 g/9 oz haddock fillets,
skinned

200 g/7 oz prawns, peeled
and deveined

100 g/3^1/$_2$ oz scallops

salt and pepper

fresh baguettes, to serve

method

1 Heat the oil in a large saucepan over a medium heat. Add the garlic and onions and cook, stirring, for 3 minutes. Stir in the tomatoes, stock, wine, bay leaf, saffron and herbs. Bring to the boil, reduce the heat, cover and simmer for 30 minutes.

2 Meanwhile, soak the mussels in lightly salted water for 10 minutes. Scrub the shells under cold running water and pull off any beards. Discard any with broken shells. Tap the remaining mussels and discard any that refuse to close. Put the rest into a large saucepan with a little water, bring to the boil and cook over a high heat for 4 minutes. Remove from the heat and discard any that remain closed.

3 When the tomato mixture is cooked, rinse the fish, pat dry and cut into chunks. Add to the pan and simmer for 5 minutes. Add the mussels, prawns and scallops, and season. Cook for 3 minutes, until the fish is cooked through. Remove from the heat, discard the bay leaf and ladle into serving bowls. Serve with fresh baguettes.

tunisian garlic & chickpea soup

ingredients

SERVES 4

8 tbsp olive oil

12 garlic cloves,
    very finely chopped

350 g/12 oz dried chickpeas,
    soaked overnight in cold
    water and drained

2.5 litres/4$^{1}/_{2}$ pints water

1 tsp ground cumin

1 tsp ground coriander

2 carrots, very finely chopped

2 onions, very finely chopped

6 celery sticks, very finely
    chopped

juice of 1 lemon

salt and pepper

4 tbsp chopped fresh
    coriander

method

1 Heat half the oil in a large, heavy-based saucepan. Add the garlic and cook over a low heat, stirring frequently, for 2 minutes. Add the chickpeas to the pan with the measured water, cumin and ground coriander. Bring to the boil, then reduce the heat and simmer for 2$^{1}/_{2}$ hours, or until tender.

2 Meanwhile, heat the remaining oil in a separate saucepan. Add the carrots, onions and celery. Cover and cook over a medium–low heat, stirring occasionally, for 20 minutes.

3 Stir the vegetable mixture into the pan of chickpeas. Transfer about half the soup to a food processor or blender and process until smooth. Return the purée to the pan, add about half the lemon juice and stir. Taste and add more lemon juice as required. Season with salt and pepper. Ladle into warmed bowls, sprinkle with the fresh coriander and serve.

cracked marinated olives

ingredients

SERVES 8

450 g/1 lb can or jar
   unstoned large green
   olives, drained
4 garlic cloves, peeled
2 tsp coriander seeds
1 small lemon
4 sprigs of fresh thyme
4 feathery stalks of fennel
2 small fresh red chillies
   (optional)
pepper
Spanish extra virgin olive oil,
   to cover

method

1 To allow the flavours of the marinade to penetrate the olives, place on a cutting board and, using a rolling pin, bash them lightly so that they crack slightly. Alternatively, use a sharp knife to cut a lengthways slit in each olive as far as the stone. Using the flat side of a broad knife, lightly crush each garlic clove. Using a mortar and pestle, crack the coriander seeds. Cut the lemon, with its rind, into small chunks.

2 Put the olives, garlic, coriander seeds, lemon chunks, thyme sprigs, fennel and chillies, if using, in a large bowl and toss together. Season with pepper to taste, but you should not need to add salt as preserved olives are usually salty enough. Pack the ingredients tightly into a glass jar with a lid. Pour in enough olive oil to cover the olives, then seal the jar tightly.

3 Let the olives stand at room temperature for 24 hours, then marinate in the refrigerator for at least a week, but preferably 2 weeks, before serving. From time to time, gently give the jar a shake to remix the ingredients. Return the olives to room temperature and remove from the oil to serve. Provide cocktail sticks for spearing the olives.

tapenade

ingredients

**MAKES ABOUT
300 G/10½ OZ**

250 g/9 oz black olives, such
   as Nyons or Niçoise,
   stoned

3 anchovy fillets in oil,
   drained

1 large garlic clove, halved,
   with the green centre
   removed if necessary

2 tbsp pine kernels

½ tbsp capers in brine,
   rinsed

125 ml/4 fl oz extra virgin
   olive oil

freshly squeezed lemon or
   orange juice, to taste

pepper

garlic croûtes

12 slices French bread, about
   5 mm/¼ inch thick

extra virgin olive oil

2 garlic cloves, peeled
   and halved

method

1 Put the olives, anchovy fillets, garlic, pine kernels and capers in a food processor or blender and whiz until well blended. With the motor still running, pour the olive oil through the feed tube and continue blending until a loose paste forms.

2 Add the lemon juice and pepper to taste. It shouldn't need any salt because of the saltiness of the anchovies. Cover and chill until required.

3 To make the garlic croûtes, preheat the grill to high. Place the bread slices on the grill rack and toast 1 side for 1–2 minutes, or until golden brown. Flip the bread slices over, lightly brush the untoasted side with olive oil, then toast for 1–2 minutes.

4 Rub 1 side of each bread slice with the garlic cloves while it is still hot, then set aside and cool completely. Store in an airtight container for up to 2 days.

5 Serve the tapenade with the garlic croûtes.

hummus

ingredients

SERVES 4

115 g/4 oz dried chickpeas

3–6 tbsp lemon juice

3–6 tbsp water

2–3 garlic cloves, crushed

150 ml/5 fl oz tahini

salt

1 tbsp olive oil

1 tsp cayenne pepper or
    paprika

1 fresh flat-leaf parsley sprig,
    to garnish

to serve

pitta bread

fresh salad leaves

slices of fresh tomato

method

1 Soak the chickpeas overnight in enough cold water to cover them and allow room for expansion. Drain the chickpeas, place them in a saucepan, cover with fresh cold water, bring to the boil, then let boil for about 1 hour, or until tender. Remove from the heat and drain.

2 Place the chickpeas in a food processor and blend with enough lemon juice and water to make a thick, smooth paste.

3 Add the garlic cloves and mix well. Add the tahini and salt to taste. Add more lemon juice or water, if necessary, to get the flavour and consistency that you want.

4 Spoon into a serving dish, drizzle over the oil and sprinkle with either cayenne pepper or paprika.

5 Cover with clingfilm and chill for at least 1 hour before serving. Garnish with a fresh parsley sprig and serve with pitta bread, fresh salad leaves and slices of tomato.

baba ghanoush with flat breads

ingredients

SERVES 4–6

1 large aubergine, pricked all
    over with a fork

3 fat garlic cloves, unpeeled

1 tsp ground coriander

1 tsp ground cumin

1 tbsp light tahini

juice of $1/2$ lemon

2 tbsp extra virgin olive oil

salt and pepper

fresh coriander, to garnish

flat breads

250 g/9 oz strong white flour,
    plus extra for dusting

2 tbsp fine cornmeal

1 tsp baking powder

1 tsp salt

scant 4 tbsp butter, diced

150–175 ml/5–6 fl oz warm
    water

corn oil, for oiling

method

1 Bake the aubergine in a roasting tin in a preheated oven, 200°C/400°F/Gas Mark 6, for 25 minutes. Add the garlic cloves and cook for 15 minutes until the aubergine and garlic are very tender.

2 Halve the aubergine and scoop the flesh into a food processor. Peel the garlic cloves and add to the aubergine with the spices, tahini, lemon juice and oil. Process until smooth, then season to taste. Transfer to a serving dish, garnish and cover until required.

3 To make the flat breads, sift the flour, cornmeal, baking powder and salt into a mixing bowl, then rub in the butter until the mixture resembles breadcrumbs. Stir in the water, first with a wooden spoon, then with your hands to bring the mixture together into a ball.

4 Turn the mixture out onto a lightly floured work surface and knead lightly until a soft dough forms. Divide into 6 pieces, then roll each into a ball. Wrap in clingfilm and let rest in the refrigerator for 30 minutes.

5 Roll out or press the dough balls with your fingers into 5-mm/$1/4$-inch-thick circles. Cook on a lightly oiled griddle pan over a medium heat for a few minutes on each side until lightly golden. Serve warm with the dip.

falafel

ingredients

SERVES 4

225 g/8 oz dried chickpeas

1 large onion, finely chopped

1 garlic clove, crushed

salt and cayenne pepper

2 tbsp chopped fresh parsley

2 tsp ground cumin

2 tsp ground coriander

$1/2$ tsp baking powder

vegetable oil, for deep-frying

hummus (see page 18) and
    pitta bread, to serve

method

1 Soak the chickpeas overnight in enough cold water to cover them and allow room for expansion. Drain the chickpeas, place them in a saucepan, cover with fresh cold water, bring to the boil, then let boil for about 1 hour, or until tender. Remove from the heat and drain.

2 Place the chickpeas in a food processor and process to make a coarse paste. Add the onion, garlic, seasoning, parsley, spices and baking powder and process again to mix.

3 Let the mixture rest for 30 minutes, then divide into 8 equal pieces. Shape each piece into a ball between the palms of your hands and arrange on a plate. Let rest for a further 30 minutes.

4 Heat the oil for deep-frying in a wok or deep pan to 180–190°C/350–375°F, or until a cube of bread browns in 30 seconds. Gently drop the balls into the oil and cook until golden brown. Carefully remove from the oil and drain for a few minutes on a plate lined with kitchen paper.

5 Serve the falafel hot or at room temperature accompanied by hummus and pitta bread.

monkfish, rosemary & bacon skewers

ingredients

SERVES 4–6

250 g/9 oz monkfish fillet

12 stalks of fresh rosemary

3 tbsp Spanish olive oil

juice of $1/2$ small lemon

1 garlic clove, crushed

salt and pepper

6 thick slices of back bacon

lemon wedges, to garnish

garlic mayonnaise, to serve

method

1 Slice the monkfish fillets in half lengthways, then cut each fillet into 12 bite-sized chunks to make a total of 24 pieces. Put the monkfish pieces in a large bowl.

2 To prepare the rosemary skewers, strip the leaves off the stalks and set them aside, leaving a few leaves at one end.

3 For the marinade, finely chop the reserved leaves and whisk together in a bowl with the olive oil, lemon juice, garlic, salt and pepper. Add the monkfish pieces and toss until coated in the marinade. Cover and marinate in the refrigerator for 1–2 hours.

4 Cut each bacon slice in half lengthways, then in half widthways, and roll up each piece. Thread 2 pieces of monkfish alternately with 2 bacon rolls onto each rosemary skewer.

5 Preheat the grill, griddle pan or barbecue. If you are cooking the skewers under a grill, arrange them on the grill pan so that the leaves of the rosemary skewers protrude from the grill and do not catch fire. Grill the monkfish and bacon skewers for 10 minutes, turning from time to time and basting with any remaining marinade, or until cooked. Serve hot, garnished with lemon wedges, with a bowl of garlic mayonnaise for dipping.

white fish & caper croquettes

ingredients

MAKES 12

350 g/12 oz white fish fillets,
    such as cod, haddock
    or monkfish, skinned
    and boned
300 ml/10 fl oz milk
salt and pepper
55 g/2 oz butter
55 g/2 oz plain flour
4 tbsp capers,
    roughly chopped
1 tsp paprika
1 garlic clove, crushed
1 tsp lemon juice
3 tbsp chopped fresh
    flat-leaf parsley, plus extra
    sprigs to garnish
1 egg, beaten
55 g/2 oz fresh white
    breadcrumbs
1 tbsp sesame seeds
corn oil, for deep-frying
lemon wedges, to garnish
mayonnaise, to serve

method

1 Put the fish fillets and milk in a large frying pan and season to taste. Bring to the boil, then lower the heat, cover the pan and cook for 8–10 minutes, or until the fish flakes easily. Remove the fish, reserving the milk. Flake the fish.

2 Heat the butter in a saucepan. Add the flour and cook gently, stirring, for 1 minute. Gradually stir in the reserved milk until smooth. Slowly bring to the boil, stirring, until the sauce thickens.

3 Remove from the heat, add the flaked fish, and beat until smooth. Add the capers, paprika, garlic, lemon juice and parsley and mix well. Season to taste. Transfer to a dish and let cool. Cover and chill for 2–3 hours.

4 Pour the beaten egg onto a plate. Combine the breadcrumbs and sesame seeds on a separate plate. Divide the fish mixture into 12 portions and form each portion into a 7.5-cm/3-inch sausage shape. Dip each croquette in the beaten egg, then coat it in the breadcrumb mixture. Chill for 1 hour.

5 Heat the oil in a deep-fryer to 180–190ºC/ 350–375ºF. Cook the croquettes, in batches, for 3 minutes, or until golden brown and crispy. Drain well on kitchen paper. Serve garnished with lemon wedges and parsley sprigs, with a bowl of mayonnaise for dipping.

tuna & tomato boreks

ingredients

MAKES 18

about 18 sheets filo pastry,
  38 x 15 cm/15 x 6 inches
  each, thawed if frozen
vegetable oil, for sealing and
  pan-frying
sea salt, to garnish
green salad and lemon
  wedges, to serve

filling

2 hard-boiled eggs, shelled
  and finely chopped
200 g/7 oz canned tuna in
  brine, drained
1 tbsp chopped fresh dill
1 tomato, peeled, deseeded
  and very finely chopped
$1/4$ tsp cayenne pepper
salt and pepper

method

1 To make the filling, put the eggs in a bowl with the tuna and dill and mash the mixture until blended.

2 Stir in the tomato, taking care not to break it up too much. Season with the cayenne pepper, salt and pepper. Set aside.

3 Lay a sheet of filo pastry out on a work surface with a short side nearest to you, keeping the remaining sheets covered with a damp tea towel. Arrange about 1 tablespoon of the filling in a line along the short side, about 1 cm/$1/2$ inch in from the end and 2.5 cm/1 inch in from both long sides.

4 Make one tight roll to enclose the filling, then fold in both long sides for the length of the filo. Continue rolling up to the end. Use a little vegetable oil to seal the end. Repeat to make 17 more rolls, or until all the filling has been used up.

5 Heat 2.5 cm/1 inch of oil in a frying pan to 180–190°C/350–375°F, or until a cube of bread browns in 30 seconds. Deep-fry 2–3 boreks at a time for 2–3 minutes until golden brown. Remove with a slotted spoon and drain well on kitchen paper. Sprinkle with sea salt. Serve hot or at room temperature with a green salad and lemon wedges for squeezing over.

calamari

ingredients

SERVES 6

450 g/1 lb prepared squid

plain flour, for coating

sunflower oil, for deep-frying

salt

lemon wedges, to garnish

garlic mayonnaise, to serve

method

1 Slice the squid into 1-cm/^{1}/$_2$-inch rings and halve the tentacles if large. Rinse under cold running water and dry well with kitchen paper. Dust the squid rings with flour so that they are lightly coated.

2 Heat the oil in a deep-fat fryer, large heavy-based saucepan, or wok to 180–190ºC/ 350–375ºF, or until a cube of bread browns in 30 seconds. Deep-fry the squid rings in small batches for 2–3 minutes, or until golden brown and crisp all over, turning several times (if you deep-fry too many squid rings at one time, the oil temperature will drop and they will be soggy). Do not overcook as the squid will become tough and rubbery rather than moist and tender.

3 Remove with a slotted spoon and drain well on kitchen paper. Keep warm in a low oven while you deep-fry the remaining squid rings.

4 Sprinkle the fried squid rings with salt and serve piping hot, garnished with lemon wedges for squeezing over. Accompany with a bowl of garlic mayonnaise for dipping.

mussels with herb & garlic butter

ingredients

SERVES 8

800 g/1 lb 12 oz live mussels

splash of dry white wine

1 bay leaf

6 tbsp butter

35 g/1³/₄ oz fresh white or
    brown breadcrumbs

4 tbsp chopped fresh flat-leaf
    parsley, plus extra sprigs
    to garnish

2 tbsp snipped fresh chives

2 garlic cloves, finely chopped

salt and pepper

lemon wedges, to serve

method

1 Clean the mussels by scrubbing or scraping the shells and pulling out any beards that are attached to them. Discard any with broken shells and any that refuse to close when tapped. Put the mussels in a colander and rinse well under cold running water.

2 Put the mussels in a large saucepan and add the wine and bay leaf. Cook, covered, over a high heat, shaking the pan occasionally, for 3–4 minutes, or until the mussels have opened. Discard any mussels that remain closed. Drain the mussels.

3 Shell the mussels, reserving one half of each shell. Arrange the mussels, in their half shells, in a large, shallow, ovenproof serving dish.

4 Melt the butter in a small saucepan and pour into a small bowl. Add the breadcrumbs, parsley, chives, garlic, salt and pepper and mix together well. Leave until the butter has set slightly. Using your fingers or 2 teaspoons, take a large pinch of the butter mixture and use to fill each mussel shell, pressing it down well.

5 Bake the mussels in a preheated oven, 230°C/450°F/Gas Mark 8, for 10 minutes, or until hot. Serve immediately, garnished with parsley sprigs, and accompanied by lemon wedges for squeezing over.

lime-drizzled prawns

ingredients

SERVES 6

4 limes

12 raw jumbo prawns, in their
    shells

3 tbsp Spanish olive oil

2 garlic cloves, finely chopped

splash of fino sherry

salt and pepper

4 tbsp chopped fresh flat-leaf
    parsley

method

1 Grate the rind and squeeze the juice from
2 of the limes. Cut the remaining 2 limes into
wedges and set aside for later.

2 To prepare the prawns, remove the heads
and legs, leaving the shells and tails intact.
Using a sharp knife, make a shallow slit along
the back of each prawn, then pull out the dark
vein and discard. Rinse the prawns under
cold water and dry on kitchen paper.

3 Heat the olive oil in a large, heavy-based
frying pan, then add the garlic and cook for
30 seconds. Add the prawns and cook for
5 minutes, stirring from time to time, or until
they turn pink and start to curl. Mix in the
lime rind and juice, add a splash of sherry to
moisten, then stir well together.

4 Transfer the cooked prawns to a serving
dish, season with salt and pepper and
sprinkle with the parsley. Serve piping hot,
accompanied by the reserved lime wedges for
squeezing over the prawns.

scallops with breadcrumbs & parsley

ingredients

SERVES 4

20 large fresh scallops,
   shucked, about
   4 cm/1¹⁄₂ inches thick
salt and pepper
200 g/7 oz clarified butter
85 g/3 oz day-old French
   bread, made into fine
   breadcrumbs
4 garlic cloves, finely chopped
5 tbsp finely chopped fresh
   flat-leaf parsley
lemon wedges, to serve

method

1 Preheat the oven to its lowest temperature. Use a small knife to remove the dark vein that runs around each scallop, then rinse and pat dry. Season to taste and set aside.

2 Melt half the butter in a large sauté pan or frying pan over a high heat. Add the breadcrumbs and garlic, then reduce the heat to medium and cook, stirring, for 5–6 minutes, or until the breadcrumbs are golden brown and crisp. Remove the breadcrumbs from the pan and drain well on kitchen paper, then keep warm in the oven. Wipe out the pan.

3 Use 2 large sauté pans or frying pans to cook all the scallops at once without overcrowding the pans. Melt 55 g/2 oz of the butter in each pan over a high heat. Reduce the heat to medium. Divide the scallops between the 2 pans in single layers; cook for 2 minutes.

4 Turn the scallops over and continue pan-frying for a further 2–3 minutes, or until they are golden and cooked through if you cut one with a knife. Add extra butter to the pans if necessary.

5 Divide the scallops between 4 warmed plates and sprinkle with the breadcrumbs and parsley mixed together. Serve with lemon wedges for squeezing over.

stuffed vine leaves

ingredients

MAKES ABOUT 30

225-g/8-oz packet vine leaves
     preserved in brine
115 g/4 oz arborio or other
     short-grain rice
175 ml/6 fl oz olive oil
1 small onion, finely chopped
1 garlic clove, finely chopped
55 g/2 oz pine kernels,
     chopped
55 g/2 oz currants
3 spring onions, finely
     chopped
1 tbsp chopped fresh mint
1 tbsp chopped fresh dill
2 tbsp chopped fresh flat-leaf
     parsley
salt and pepper
juice of 1 lemon
lemon wedges and Greek-
     style yogurt, to serve

method

1 Place the vine leaves in a bowl, add boiling water and soak for 20 minutes. Drain, soak in cold water for 20 minutes and drain again.

2 Meanwhile, cover the rice with cold water in a saucepan, bring to the boil, then simmer for 15–20 minutes, or until tender. Drain well and set aside in a bowl to cool.

3 Heat 2 tablespoons of the oil in a frying pan and fry the onion and garlic until softened. Add to the rice with the pine kernels, currants, spring onions, mint, dill and parsley. Season with a little salt and plenty of pepper, and mix well.

4 Place one vine leaf, vein-side upward, on a work surface. Put a little filling on the base of the leaf and fold up the bottom end of the leaf. Fold in the sides, then roll up the leaf around the filling. Squeeze gently to seal. Fill and roll the remaining leaves, then pack the stuffed leaves close together in a large flameproof casserole, seam-side down and in a single layer.

5 Mix the remaining oil and the lemon juice with 150 ml/5 fl oz water and pour into the casserole. Place a large plate over the vine leaves to keep them in place then cover the casserole with a lid. Bring to simmering point, then simmer for 45 minutes. Leave the vine leaves to cool in the liquid.

6 Serve warm or chilled, with lemon wedges and yogurt.

artichokes with vièrge sauce

ingredients

SERVES 4

4 large globe artichokes
1/2 lemon, sliced
salt

vièrge sauce

3 large beefsteak tomatoes,
   peeled and deseeded,
   then finely diced
4 spring onions, very finely
   chopped
6 tbsp chopped fresh herbs,
   such as basil, chervil,
   chives, mint, flat-leaf
   parsley or tarragon
150 ml/5 fl oz full-flavoured
   extra virgin olive oil
pinch of sugar
salt and pepper

method

1 To prepare the artichokes, cut off the stems and trim the bottom so that they will stand upright on the plate. Use scissors to snip the leaf tips off each artichoke, then drop in a large bowl of water with 2 of the lemon slices while the others are being prepared.

2 Meanwhile, select a saucepan large enough to hold all 4 artichokes upright and half-fill with salted water and the remaining lemon slices. Bring the water to the boil, then add the artichokes and place a heatproof plate on top to keep them submerged. Reduce the heat to a low boil and continue boiling the artichokes for 25–35 minutes, depending on their size, until the bottom leaves pull out easily.

3 While the artichokes are cooking, prepare the vièrge sauce. Put the tomatoes, spring onions, herbs, oil, sugar, salt and pepper in a pan and set aside for the flavours to blend.

4 When the artichokes are tender, drain them upside-down on kitchen paper, then transfer to individual plates. Heat the sauce very gently until it is just warm, then spoon it equally over the artichokes.

asparagus with hollandaise sauce

ingredients

SERVES 4

650 g/1 lb 7 oz green
asparagus, with any woody
ends broken off and the
stalks trimmed to the
same length

hollandaise sauce

4 tbsp white wine vinegar

$1/2$ tbsp finely chopped shallot

5 black peppercorns

1 bay leaf

3 large egg yolks

140 g/5 oz unsalted butter,
finely diced

2 tsp lemon juice

salt

pinch of cayenne pepper

method

1 Divide the asparagus into 4 bundles and tie each with kitchen string, criss-crossing the string from just below the tips to the base. Stand the bundles upright in a deep saucepan. Add boiling water to come three quarters of the way up the stalks, then cover with a loose tent of foil, shiny-side down, inside the pan. Heat the water until bubbles appear around the side of the pan, then simmer for 10 minutes, or until the stalks are just tender when pierced with the tip of a knife. Drain well.

2 Meanwhile, to make the hollandaise sauce, boil the vinegar, shallot, peppercorns and bay leaf in a saucepan over a high heat until reduced to 1 tablespoon. Cool slightly, then strain into a heatproof bowl that will fit over a saucepan of simmering water without touching the water.

3 Beat the egg yolks into the bowl. Set the bowl over the pan of simmering water and whisk the egg yolks constantly until they are thick enough to leave a trail on the surface. Do not let the water boil. Gradually beat in the butter, piece by piece, whisking constantly until the sauce is like soft mayonnaise. Stir in the lemon juice, then add salt to taste and the cayenne pepper. Serve the sauce immediately with the asparagus.

sicilian stuffed tomatoes

ingredients

SERVES 4

8 large, ripe tomatoes

7 tbsp extra virgin olive oil

2 onions, finely chopped

2 garlic cloves, crushed

115 g/4 oz fresh
breadcrumbs

8 anchovy fillets in oil,
drained and chopped

3 tbsp black olives, stoned
and chopped

2 tbsp chopped fresh flat-leaf
parsley

1 tbsp chopped fresh oregano

4 tbsp freshly grated
Parmesan cheese

method

1 Cut a thin slice off the top of each tomato and discard. Scoop out the seeds with a teaspoon and discard, taking care not to pierce the shell. Turn the tomato shells upside down on kitchen paper to drain.

2 Heat 6 tablespoons of the olive oil in a frying pan, add the onions and garlic and cook over a low heat, stirring occasionally, for 5 minutes, until softened. Remove the pan from the heat and stir in the breadcrumbs, anchovies, olives and herbs.

3 Using a teaspoon, fill the tomato shells with the breadcrumb mixture, then place in an ovenproof dish large enough to hold them in a single layer. Sprinkle the tops with grated Parmesan and drizzle with the remaining oil.

4 Bake in a preheated oven, 180°C/350°F/Gas Mark 4, for 20–25 minutes, until the tomatoes are tender and the topping is golden brown.

5 Remove the dish from the oven and serve immediately, if serving hot, or cool to room temperature.

meat &
poultry

Meat is enjoyed in all Mediterranean countries, although not necessarily in great quantities. Roast lamb, a particular favourite, is served on festive occasions such as Easter and marries well with the herb rosemary, which grows wild and profusely. Try Roast Lamb with Rosemary & Marsala for the Italian twist – the pan juices are reduced to a thick, syrupy, delicious sauce to serve with the lamb. In Morocco, lamb is served as a 'tagine', an unusual dish, cooked with vegetables and apricots, which is low in fat, high in flavour and excellent served with couscous.

Meat is often transformed into sausages – try Sausages with Lentils, a Spanish dish that uses spicy lamb or beef merguez sausages, but which can also be made with pork or wild boar sausages. Chickens are raised in all Mediterranean countries, and are often free-range, so have an excellent flavour. In Greece, where chickens are often seen happily foraging on country roadsides, they are used in a pie with crisp, flaky filo pastry, and Chicken Kebabs with Yogurt Sauce is served in most Greek tavernas. In France, Chicken in Tarragon Sauce is a classic dish – the sauce is rich, creamy and full of flavour.

Paella is a speciality of Spain. This is definitely a treat to try!

roast lamb with rosemary & marsala

ingredients

SERVES 6

1.8 kg/4 lb leg of lamb
2 garlic cloves, thinly sliced
2 tbsp rosemary leaves
8 tbsp olive oil
salt and pepper
900 g/2 lb potatoes, cut into
   2.5-cm/1-inch cubes
6 fresh sage leaves, chopped
125 ml/4 fl oz Marsala

method

1 Use a small, sharp knife to make incisions all over the lamb, opening them out slightly to make little pockets. Insert the garlic slices and about half the rosemary leaves in the pockets.

2 Place the lamb in a roasting tin and spoon half the olive oil over it. Roast in a preheated oven, 220°C/425°F/Gas Mark 7, for 15 minutes. Reduce the oven temperature to 180°C/350°F/Gas Mark 4. Remove the lamb from the oven and season to taste. Turn the lamb over, return to the oven and roast for a further hour.

3 Meanwhile, spread out the cubed potatoes in a second roasting tin, pour the remaining olive oil over them and toss to coat. Sprinkle with the remaining rosemary and the sage. Place the potatoes in the oven with the lamb, and roast for 40 minutes.

4 Remove the lamb from the oven, turn it over and pour over the Marsala. Return it to the oven with the potatoes and cook for a further 15 minutes.

5 Transfer the lamb to a carving board and cover with foil. Place the roasting tin over a low heat, bring the juices to the boil and boil until thickened and syrupy, then strain. Carve the lamb into slices and serve with the potatoes and sauce.

provençal barbecued lamb

ingredients

SERVES 4–6

1 leg of lamb, about
    1.5 kg/3 lb 5 oz, boned
olive oil, for brushing

marinade

1 bottle full-bodied red wine
2 large garlic cloves, chopped
2 tbsp extra virgin olive oil
large handful of fresh rosemary
    sprigs, plus extra to garnish
fresh thyme sprigs, plus extra
    to garnish

black olive tapenade

250 g/9 oz black olives in
    brine, rinsed and stoned
1 large garlic clove
2 tbsp walnut pieces
4 canned anchovy fillets,
    drained
125 ml/4 fl oz extra virgin
    olive oil
lemon juice, to taste
pepper

method

1 Place the lamb on a cutting board. Holding the knife almost flat, slice horizontally into the pocket left by the leg bone, taking care not to cut all the way through, so the meat can be opened out flat. Place in a large non-metallic bowl and add the marinade ingredients. Cover with clingfilm and marinate in the refrigerator for 24 hours, turning several times.

2 To make the tapenade, blend the olives, garlic, walnut pieces and anchovies in a food processor. With the motor running, slowly add the olive oil through the feed tube. Add lemon juice and pepper to taste. Transfer to a bowl, cover and chill until required.

3 Remove the lamb from the marinade and pat dry. Lay the lamb flat and thread 2–3 long metal skewers through the flesh, so that the meat remains flat while it cooks. Spread the tapenade all over the lamb on both sides.

4 Brush the barbecue rack with oil. Place the lamb on the rack about 10 cm/4 inches above hot coals and cook for 5 minutes. Turn and cook for a further 5 minutes. Turn twice more at 5-minute intervals. Raise the rack if the meat begins to look charred – it should be medium-cooked after 20–25 minutes.

5 Remove the lamb from the heat and let stand for 10 minutes. Carve into thin slices and garnish with rosemary and thyme sprigs.

marinated lamb & vegetable kebabs

ingredients

SERVES 4

juice of 2 large lemons

100 ml/3¹/₂ fl oz olive oil, plus
extra for oiling

1 garlic clove, crushed

1 tbsp chopped fresh oregano
or mint

salt and pepper

700 g/1 lb 9 oz boned leg or
fillet of lamb, trimmed and
cut into 4-cm/1¹/₂-inch
cubes

2 green peppers

2 courgettes

12 pearl onions, peeled and
left whole

8 large bay leaves

lemon wedges, to garnish

rice, to serve

cucumber & yogurt dip

1 small cucumber

300 ml/10 fl oz Greek-style
yogurt

1 large garlic clove, crushed

1 tbsp chopped fresh mint
or dill

salt and pepper

method

1 To make the cucumber and yogurt dip, peel then coarsely grate the cucumber. Put in a sieve and squeeze out as much of the water as possible. Put the cucumber into a bowl. Add the yogurt, garlic and chopped mint, season with pepper and mix thoroughly. Chill in the refrigerator for 2 hours. Sprinkle with salt just before serving.

2 Put the lemon juice, oil, garlic, oregano, salt and pepper in a bowl and whisk together. Add the lamb to the marinade.

3 Toss the lamb in the marinade, cover and refrigerate overnight or for at least 8 hours. Stir occasionally to coat the lamb.

4 When ready to serve, core and deseed the peppers, and cut into 4-cm/1¹/₂-inch pieces. Cut the courgettes into 2.5-cm/1-inch pieces. Thread the lamb, peppers, courgettes, onions and bay leaves onto 8 flat, oiled metal kebab skewers, alternating and dividing the ingredients as evenly as possible. Place on an oiled grill pan.

5 Cook the kebabs under a preheated grill for 10–15 minutes, turning frequently and basting with any remaining marinade. Serve hot, garnished with lemon wedges, with rice and the cucumber and yogurt dip.

tagine of lamb

ingredients

SERVES 4

1 tbsp sunflower or
    corn oil
1 onion, chopped
350 g/12 oz boneless lamb,
    trimmed of all visible fat
    and cut into 2.5-cm/
    1-inch cubes
1 garlic clove, finely chopped
600 ml/1 pint vegetable stock
grated rind and juice of
    1 orange
1 tsp clear honey
1 cinnamon stick
1-cm/$1/2$-inch piece fresh
    ginger, finely chopped
1 aubergine
4 tomatoes, peeled and
    chopped
115 g/4 oz no-soak dried
    apricots
2 tbsp chopped fresh
    coriander
salt and pepper
freshly cooked couscous,
    to serve

method

1 Heat the oil in a large, flameproof casserole over a medium heat. Add the onion and lamb cubes and cook, stirring frequently, for 5 minutes, or until the meat is lightly browned all over. Add the garlic, stock, orange rind and juice, honey, cinnamon stick and ginger. Bring to the boil, then reduce the heat, cover and simmer for 45 minutes.

2 Using a sharp knife, halve the aubergine lengthways and slice thinly. Add to the frying pan with the chopped tomatoes and apricots. Cover and cook for a further 45 minutes, or until the lamb is tender.

3 Stir in the coriander and season with salt and pepper. Serve immediately accompanied by freshly cooked couscous.

lamb with tomatoes, artichokes & olives

ingredients

SERVES 4

4 tbsp Greek-style yogurt

grated rind of 1 lemon

2 garlic cloves, crushed

3 tbsp olive oil

1 tsp ground cumin

salt and pepper

700 g/1 lb 9 oz lean boneless
　　lamb, cubed

1 onion, thinly sliced

150 ml/5 fl oz dry white wine

450 g/1 lb tomatoes,
　　roughly chopped

1 tbsp tomato paste

pinch of sugar

2 tbsp chopped fresh oregano
　　or 1 tsp dried

2 bay leaves

85 g/3 oz kalamata olives

400 g/14 oz canned artichoke
　　hearts, drained and halved

method

1 Put the yogurt, lemon rind, garlic, 1 tablespoon of the olive oil, the cumin, salt and pepper in a large bowl and mix together. Add the lamb and toss together until coated in the mixture. Cover and marinate for at least 1 hour.

2 Heat 1 tablespoon of the olive oil in a large flameproof casserole. Add the lamb in batches and fry for about 5 minutes, stirring frequently, until browned on all sides. Using a slotted spoon, remove the meat from the casserole and set aside. Add the remaining tablespoon of oil to the casserole with the onion and fry for 5 minutes, until softened.

3 Pour the wine into the casserole, stirring in any glazed bits from the bottom, and bring to the boil. Reduce the heat and return the meat to the casserole, then stir in the tomatoes, tomato paste, sugar, oregano and bay leaves.

4 Cover the casserole with a lid and simmer for about 1^{1}/2 hours, until the lamb is tender. Stir in the olives and artichokes and simmer for another 10 minutes. Serve hot.

moussaka

ingredients

SERVES 4

2 aubergines, thinly sliced

450 g/1 lb fresh lean
    beef mince

2 onions, thinly sliced

1 tsp finely chopped garlic

400 g/14 oz canned tomatoes

2 tbsp chopped fresh parsley

salt and pepper

2 eggs

300 ml/10 fl oz Greek-style
    yogurt

1 tbsp freshly grated
    Parmesan cheese

method

1 Dry-fry the aubergine slices, in batches, in a non-stick frying pan on both sides until browned. Remove from the pan.

2 Add the beef to the frying pan and cook for 5 minutes, stirring, until browned. Stir in the onions and garlic and cook for 5 minutes, or until browned. Add the tomatoes, parsley, salt and pepper, then bring to the boil and simmer for 20 minutes, or until the meat is tender.

3 Arrange half the aubergine slices in a layer in an ovenproof dish. Add the meat mixture, then a final layer of the remaining aubergine slices.

4 Beat the eggs in a bowl, then beat in the yogurt and season with salt and pepper. Pour the mixture over the aubergines and sprinkle the grated cheese on top. Bake the moussaka in a preheated oven, 180°C/350°F/ Gas Mark 4, for 45 minutes, or until golden brown. Serve straight from the dish.

italian marinated pork chops

ingredients

SERVES 4

4 pork rib chops
4 fresh sage leaves
2 tbsp salted capers
2 gherkins, chopped
small salad, to garnish
garlic bread (optional), to
    serve

marinade

4 tbsp dry white wine
1 tbsp brown sugar
2 tbsp olive oil
1 tsp Dijon mustard

method

1 Trim any visible fat from the chops and place them in a large, shallow dish. Top each with a sage leaf. Rub the salt off the capers with your fingers and sprinkle them over the chops, together with the gherkins.

2 Mix the wine, sugar, oil and mustard together in a small bowl and pour the mixture over the chops. Cover with clingfilm and marinate in a cool place for about 2 hours.

3 Drain the chops, reserving the marinade. Cook the chops on a hot barbecue for 5 minutes on each side, then over medium coals or on a higher rack, turning and brushing occasionally with the reserved marinade, for about 10 minutes more on each side, or until cooked through and tender.

4 Serve immediately with a small salad and garlic bread if you like.

sausages with lentils

ingredients

SERVES 4–6

2 tbsp olive oil

12 merguez sausages

2 onions, finely chopped

2 red peppers, cored,
   deseeded and chopped

1 orange or yellow pepper,
   cored, deseeded and
   chopped

280 g/10 oz small green
   lentils, rinsed

1 tsp dried thyme or marjoram

500 ml/18 fl oz vegetable
   stock

salt and pepper

4 tbsp chopped fresh parsley

red wine vinegar, to serve

method

1 Heat the oil in a large, preferably non-stick, lidded frying pan over a medium–high heat. Add the sausages and cook, stirring frequently, for about 10 minutes until they are brown all over and cooked through; remove from the pan and set aside.

2 Pour off all but 2 tablespoons of oil from the frying pan. Add the onions and peppers and cook for about 5 minutes until soft, but not brown. Add the lentils and thyme and stir until coated with oil.

3 Stir in the stock and bring to the boil. Reduce the heat, cover and simmer for about 30 minutes until the lentils are tender and the liquid is absorbed; if the lentils are tender but too much liquid remains, uncover the pan and simmer until it evaporates. Season with salt and pepper.

4 Return the sausages to the frying pan and reheat. Stir in the parsley. Serve the sausages with the lentils, then splash a little red wine vinegar over each portion.

greek-style beef kebabs

ingredients

SERVES 4–6

1 small onion, finely chopped

1 tbsp chopped fresh
    coriander

large pinch of paprika

$1/4$ tsp ground allspice

$1/4$ tsp ground coriander

$1/4$ tsp brown sugar

450 g/1 lb beef mince

salt and pepper

vegetable oil, for brushing

fresh coriander leaves, to
    garnish

freshly cooked bulgar wheat
    or rice, and mixed salad,
    to serve

method

1 If you are using wooden skewers, soak them in cold water for 30 minutes before use.

2 Put the onion, fresh coriander, spices, sugar and beef into a large bowl and mix until well combined. Season with salt and pepper.

3 On a clean work surface, use your hands to shape the mixture into sausages around skewers. Brush them lightly with vegetable oil.

4 Grill the kebabs over hot coals, turning them frequently, for 15–20 minutes, or until cooked right through. Arrange the kebabs on a platter of freshly cooked bulgar wheat and garnish with fresh coriander leaves. Serve with a mixed salad.

osso bucco with citrus rinds

ingredients

MAKES 12

1–2 tbsp plain flour

salt and pepper

6 meaty slices osso bucco
   (veal shins)

1–2 tbsp olive oil

250 g/9 oz onions, very finely
   chopped

250 g/9 oz carrots, finely diced

1 kg/2 lb 4 oz fresh tomatoes,
   peeled, deseeded and
   diced, or 800 g/1 lb 12
   oz canned chopped
   tomatoes, drained and
   passed through a sieve

250 ml/8 fl oz dry white wine

250 ml/8 fl oz veal stock

6 large basil leaves, torn

1 large garlic clove, very finely
   chopped

finely grated rind of 1 large
   lemon

finely grated rind of 1 orange

2 tbsp finely chopped fresh
   flat-leaf parsley

crusty bread, to serve

method

1 Place the flour in a plastic bag and season with salt and pepper. Add the osso bucco, a couple of pieces at a time, and shake until well coated. Remove and shake off the excess flour. Continue until all the pieces are coated.

2 Heat 1 tablespoon of the oil in a large ovenproof casserole. Add the osso bucco and cook for 10 minutes on each slide until well browned. Remove from the casserole.

3 Add 1–2 teaspoons of oil to the casserole if necessary. Add the onions and cook for 5 minutes, stirring, until softened. Stir in the carrots and continue cooking until they become soft.

4 Add the tomatoes, wine, stock and basil and return the osso bucco to the casserole. Bring to the boil, then reduce the heat, cover and simmer for 1 hour. With the tip of a knife, check that the meat is tender. If not, continue cooking for a further 10 minutes and test again.

5 When the meat is tender, sprinkle with the garlic, lemon rind and orange rind, re-cover, and cook for a further 10 minutes. Adjust the seasoning if necessary. Sprinkle with the parsley and serve with crusty bread.

paella primavera

ingredients

SERVES 4–6

$^1/_2$ tsp saffron threads

2 tbsp hot water

3 tbsp olive oil

175 g/6 oz serrano ham,
 diced

1 large carrot, diced

150 g/5$^1/_2$ oz button
 mushrooms

4 large spring onions, diced

2 garlic cloves, crushed

1 tsp paprika

$^1/_4$ tsp cayenne pepper

225 g/8 oz tomatoes, peeled
 and cut into wedges

1 red pepper, halved and
 deseeded, then grilled,
 peeled and sliced

1 green pepper, halved and
 deseeded, then grilled,
 peeled and sliced

350 g/12 oz medium-grain
 paella rice

2 tbsp chopped mixed fresh
 herbs, plus extra to garnish

100 ml/3$^1/_2$ fl oz white wine

1.25 litres/2 pints simmering
 chicken stock

55 g/2 oz shelled peas

100 g/3$^1/_2$ oz fresh asparagus
 spears, blanched

salt and pepper

lemon wedges, to serve

method

1 Put the saffron threads and water in a small bowl to infuse for a few minutes.

2 Heat 2 tablespoons of the oil in a paella pan and cook the ham over a medium heat, stirring, for 5 minutes. Transfer to a bowl. Heat the remaining oil in the pan and cook the carrot, stirring, for 3 minutes. Add the mushrooms and cook, stirring, for 2 minutes. Add the spring onions, garlic, paprika, cayenne pepper, and saffron and its soaking liquid and cook, stirring, for 1 minute. Add the tomatoes and peppers and cook, stirring, for 2 minutes.

3 Add the rice and herbs and cook, stirring, for 1 minute, to coat the rice. Pour in the wine and most of the hot stock and bring to the boil, then simmer, uncovered, for 10 minutes. Do not stir during cooking, but shake the pan once or twice and when adding ingredients. Add the peas and season to taste. Cook for 10 minutes, or until the rice is almost cooked, adding a little more stock if necessary. Return the ham and any juices to the pan. Arrange the asparagus around the paella in a wheel pattern and cook for 2 minutes.

4 When all the liquid has been absorbed and you detect a faint toasty aroma coming from the rice, remove from the heat. Cover with foil and let stand for 5 minutes. Sprinkle over chopped herbs to garnish and serve with lemon wedges.

moroccan chicken

ingredients

SERVES 4

4 skinless, boneless chicken
  breasts, about 140 g/5
  oz each
salt and pepper
toasted flat breads, to serve

marinade

3 tbsp olive oil
4 tbsp lemon juice
2 tbsp chopped fresh parsley
2 tbsp chopped fresh
  coriander
1 garlic clove, finely chopped
1 tsp ground coriander
$1/2$ tsp ground cumin
1 tsp sweet paprika
pinch of chilli powder

salad

200 g/7 oz raw carrots
200 g/7 oz raw white cabbage
100 g/$3^1/2$ oz sprouting beans
50 g/$1^3/4$ oz alfalfa sprouts
50 g/$1^3/4$ oz sultanas
50 g/$1^3/4$ oz raisins
1 tbsp lemon juice

method

1 Mix together the oil, lemon juice, parsley, fresh coriander, garlic, ground coriander, cumin, paprika and chilli powder in a large, shallow, non-metallic dish.

2 Using a sharp knife, score the chicken breasts 3–4 times. Add the chicken to the dish, turning to coat. Cover with clingfilm and marinate in a cool place, turning occasionally, for 2–3 hours.

3 Drain the chicken, reserving the marinade. Barbecue over hot coals, brushing occasionally with the reserved marinade, for 20–30 minutes, or until tender and cooked through. Season with salt and pepper.

4 Meanwhile, to make the salad, trim and peel the carrots, then grate them into a large salad bowl. Trim the white cabbage, then shred it finely. Transfer it to a large colander and rinse under cold running water. Drain well, then add it to the carrots. Put the sprouting beans and alfalfa sprouts into the colander and rinse well, then drain and add to the salad. Rinse and drain the sultanas and raisins and add them to the bowl. Pour in the lemon juice and toss the salad into it.

5 Serve the Moroccan chicken with the salad and toasted flat breads.

chicken tagine

ingredients

SERVES 4

1 tbsp olive oil

1 onion, cut into small wedges

2–4 garlic cloves, sliced

450 g/1 lb skinless, boneless
chicken breast, diced

1 tsp ground cumin

2 cinnamon sticks, lightly
bruised

1 tbsp plain wholemeal flour

225 g/8 oz aubergine, diced

1 red pepper, deseeded and
chopped

85 g/3 oz button mushrooms,
sliced

1 tbsp tomato paste

600 ml/1 pint chicken stock

280 g/10 oz canned chickpeas,
drained and rinsed

55 g/2 oz ready-to-eat dried
apricots, chopped

salt and pepper

1 tbsp chopped fresh
coriander

method

1 Heat the oil in a large saucepan over a medium heat, add the onion and garlic and cook for 3 minutes, stirring frequently. Add the chicken and cook, stirring constantly, for a further 5 minutes, or until sealed on all sides. Add the cumin and cinnamon sticks to the pan halfway through sealing the chicken.

2 Sprinkle in the flour and cook, stirring constantly, for 2 minutes. Add the aubergine, red pepper and mushrooms and cook for a further 2 minutes, stirring constantly.

3 Blend the tomato paste with the stock, stir into the pan and bring to the boil. Reduce the heat and add the chickpeas and apricots. Cover and simmer for 15–20 minutes, or until the chicken is tender.

4 Season with salt and pepper and serve immediately, sprinkled with coriander.

spanish chicken with preserved lemons

ingredients

SERVES 4

1 tbsp plain flour

4 chicken quarters, skin on

2 tbsp olive oil

2 garlic cloves, crushed

1 large Spanish onion, thinly
   sliced

700 ml/1¼ pints chicken
   stock

½ tsp saffron threads

2 yellow peppers, deseeded
   and cut into chunks

2 preserved lemons, cut into
   quarters

250 g/9 oz brown basmati
   rice

white pepper

12 pimiento-stuffed green
   olives

chopped fresh parsley,
   to garnish

method

1 Put the flour into a large freezer bag. Add the chicken, close the top of the bag, and shake to coat with flour.

2 Heat the oil in a large frying pan over a low heat, add the garlic and cook for 1 minute, stirring constantly. Add the chicken to the pan and cook over a medium heat, turning frequently, for 5 minutes, or until the skin has lightly browned, then remove to a plate. Add the onion to the pan and cook, stirring occasionally, for 10 minutes, or until soft.

3 Meanwhile, put the stock and saffron into a saucepan over a low heat and heat through.

4 Transfer the chicken and onion to a large casserole dish, add the yellow peppers, lemons and rice, then pour over the stock. Mix well and season with pepper.

5 Cover and cook in a preheated oven, 180°C/350°F/Gas Mark 4, for 50 minutes, or until the chicken is cooked through and tender. Reduce the oven temperature to 160°C/325°F/Gas Mark 3. Add the olives to the casserole and cook for a further 10 minutes.

6 Serve sprinkled with chopped parsley.

chicken in tarragon sauce

ingredients

SERVES 4

4 boneless chicken breasts,
about 175 g/6 oz each
salt and pepper
30 g/1 oz unsalted butter
1 tbsp sunflower oil

tarragon sauce

2 tbsp tarragon-flavoured
vinegar
6 tbsp dry white wine
250 ml/9 fl oz chicken stock
4 sprigs of fresh tarragon,
plus 2 tbsp chopped
fresh tarragon
300 ml/10 fl oz soured cream
or double cream

method

1 Season the chicken breasts on both sides with salt and pepper. Over a medium–high heat, melt the butter with the oil in a frying pan large enough to hold the chicken pieces in a single layer. Add the chicken breasts, skin-side down, and sauté until golden brown.

2 Transfer the chicken breasts to a roasting tin and roast in a preheated oven, 190°C/375°F/ Gas Mark 5, for 15–20 minutes, or until they are tender and the juices run clear when a skewer is inserted into the thickest part of the meat. Transfer the chicken to a serving platter and cover with foil, shiny-side down, then set aside.

3 To make the tarragon sauce, skim the excess fat from the cooking juices. Place the roasting tin over a medium–high heat and add the vinegar, scraping any sediment from the bottom of the tin. Pour in the wine and bring to the boil, still stirring and scraping, and boil until the liquid is reduced by half.

4 Stir in the stock and whole tarragon sprigs and continue boiling until the liquid reduces to about 125 ml/4 fl oz. Stir in the soured cream and continue boiling to reduce the sauce by half. Discard the tarragon sprigs, and adjust the seasoning if necessary. Stir the chopped tarragon into the sauce.

5 To serve, slice the chicken breasts on individual plates and spoon over the sauce.

filo chicken pie

ingredients

SERVES 6

1.5 kg/3 lb 5 oz whole
    chicken
1 small onion, halved,
    and 3 large onions, finely
    chopped
1 carrot, thickly sliced
1 celery stick, thickly sliced
pared rind of 1 lemon
1 bay leaf
10 peppercorns
150 g/5$^{1}/_{2}$ oz butter
55 g/2 oz plain flour
150 ml/5 fl oz milk
salt and pepper
25 g/1 oz kefalotiri or romano
    cheese, grated
3 eggs, beaten
225 g/8 oz filo pastry (work
    with one sheet at a time
    and keep the remaining
    sheets covered with a
    damp tea towel)

method

1 Put the chicken in a large saucepan with the halved onion, carrot, celery, lemon rind, bay leaf and peppercorns. Add cold water to cover and bring to the boil. Cover and simmer for about 1 hour, or until the chicken is cooked.

2 Remove the chicken and set aside to cool. Bring the stock to the boil and boil until reduced to about 600 ml/1 pint. Strain and reserve the stock. Cut the cooled chicken into bite-sized pieces, discarding the skin and bones.

3 Fry the chopped onions until softened in 55 g/2 oz of the butter. Add the flour and cook gently, stirring, for 1–2 minutes. Gradually stir in the reserved stock and the milk. Bring to the boil, stirring constantly, then simmer for 1–2 minutes until thick and smooth. Remove from the heat, add the chicken and season. Allow to cool, then stir in the cheese and eggs.

4 Melt the remaining butter and use a little to grease a deep 30 x 20-cm/12 x 8-inch metal baking tin. Cut the pastry sheets in half widthways. Line the pan with one sheet of pastry and brush it with a little melted butter. Repeat until half of the pastry is used. Spread the filling over the pastry, then top with the remaining pastry sheets, brushing each with butter and tucking down the edges.

5 Score the top of the pie into 6 squares. Bake in a preheated oven, 190°C/375°F/Gas Mark 5, for 50 minutes, or until golden. Serve warm.

chicken kebabs with yogurt sauce

ingredients

SERVES 4

300 ml/10 fl oz Greek-style
   yogurt
2 garlic cloves, crushed
juice of $^1/_2$ lemon
1 tbsp chopped fresh herbs
   such as oregano, dill,
   tarragon or parsley
salt and pepper
4 large skinned, boned
   chicken breasts
corn oil, for oiling
8 firm stems of fresh
   rosemary, optional
lemon wedges, to garnish
shredded romaine lettuce
   and rice, to serve

method

1 To make the sauce, put the yogurt, garlic, lemon juice, herbs, salt and pepper in a large bowl and mix well together.

2 Cut the chicken breasts into chunks measuring about 4 cm/$1^1/_2$ inches square. Add to the yogurt mixture and toss well together until the chicken pieces are coated. Cover and marinate in the refrigerator for about 1 hour. If you are using wooden skewers, soak them in cold water for 30 minutes before use.

3 Preheat the grill. Thread the pieces of chicken onto 8 flat, oiled metal kebab skewers, wooden skewers or rosemary stems and place on an oiled grill pan.

4 Cook the kebabs under the grill for about 15 minutes, turning and basting with the remaining marinade occasionally, until lightly browned and tender.

5 Pour the remaining marinade into a saucepan and heat gently but do not boil. Serve the kebabs with shredded lettuce on a bed of rice, and garnish with lemon wedges. Accompany with the yogurt sauce.

pesto & ricotta chicken with tomato vinaigrette

ingredients

SERVES 4

1 tbsp pesto sauce

115 g/4 oz ricotta cheese

4 x 175 g/6 oz boneless
   chicken breasts

1 tbsp olive oil

pepper

small salad, to garnish

tomato vinaigrette

100 ml/3¹/₂ fl oz olive oil

1 bunch fresh chives

500 g/1 lb 2 oz tomatoes,
   peeled, deseeded and
   chopped

juice and finely grated rind
   of 1 lime

salt and pepper

method

1 Mix together the pesto and ricotta in a small bowl until well combined. Using a sharp knife, cut a deep slit in the side of each chicken breast to make a pocket. Spoon the ricotta mixture into the pockets and re-shape the chicken breasts to enclose it. Place the chicken on a plate, cover and chill for 30 minutes.

2 To make the vinaigrette, pour the olive oil into a blender or food processor, add the chives and process until smooth. Scrape the mixture into a bowl and stir in the tomatoes and the lime juice and rind. Season with salt and pepper.

3 Brush the chicken with the olive oil and season with pepper. Cook on a fairly hot barbecue for about 8 minutes on each side, or until cooked through and tender. Transfer to serving plates, spoon over the vinaigrette and serve immediately.

fish &
seafood

Mediterranean countries enjoy the benefits of countless miles of coastline so fish, a high-protein, low-fat food rich in vitamin B12, iron and the essential omega 3 fatty acids, is one of the key ingredients of the health-enhancing Mediterranean diet.

Fish and seafood are caught and landed every day and cooked fresh from the sea. The simplest method is to roast, grill, barbecue or pan-fry the fish with olive oil, lemon and herbs but, with such wonderful bounty at their disposal, the inhabitants of the various Mediterranean countries have become marvellously creative with their fish dishes!

Fish stews are an obvious way to use the daily catch, because a variety of fish and seafood can go into them, depending on what has been landed in the nearest harbour. Try Marseilles-style Fish Stew, a speciality of the famous French coastal town, Livornese Seafood Stew from the Tuscan port of Livorna in Italy, Spanish Swordfish Stew or Moroccan Fish Tagine.

If you prefer to keep it simple, there are some great options, such as Cod with Catalan Spinach, Grilled Red Snapper with Garlic, Chargrilled Sea Bass with Stewed Artichokes and Sicilian Tuna. They are uncomplicated and so good – try them all!

roasted monkfish

ingredients

SERVES 4

675 g/1 lb 8 oz monkfish tail, skinned

4–5 large garlic cloves, peeled

salt and pepper

3 tbsp olive oil

1 onion, cut into wedges

1 small aubergine, about 300 g/10¹/₂ oz, cut into chunks

1 red pepper, deseeded, cut into wedges

1 yellow pepper, deseeded, cut into wedges

1 large courgette, about 225 g/8 oz, cut into wedges

1 tbsp shredded fresh basil

method

1 Remove the central bone from the fish, if not already removed, and make small slits down each fillet. Cut 2 of the garlic cloves into thin slivers and insert into the fish. Place the fish on a sheet of waxed paper, season with salt and pepper and drizzle over 1 tablespoon of the oil. Bring the top edges together. Form into a pleat and fold over, then fold the ends underneath, completely encasing the fish. Set aside.

2 Put the remaining garlic cloves and all the vegetables into a roasting tin and sprinkle with the remaining oil, turning the vegetables so that they are well coated in the oil.

3 Roast in a preheated oven, 200°C/400°F/Gas Mark 6, for 20 minutes, turning occasionally. Put the fish package on top of the vegetables and cook for a further 15–20 minutes, or until the vegetables are tender and the fish is cooked.

4 Remove from the oven and open up the package. Cut the monkfish into thick slices. Arrange the vegetables on warmed serving plates, top with the fish slices and sprinkle with the basil. Serve immediately.

basque-style cod

ingredients

SERVES 4

3 tbsp olive oil

4 cod fillets, about 175 g/6 oz
    each, all skin and bones
    removed, rinsed and
    patted dry

1 tbsp plain flour

salt and pepper

1 large onion, finely chopped

4 large tomatoes, peeled,
    deseeded and chopped

2 large garlic cloves, crushed

150 ml/5 fl oz dry white wine

$1/2$ tsp paprika, to taste

2 red peppers, chargrilled,
    peeled and deseeded,
    then cut into strips

2 green peppers, chargrilled,
    peeled and deseeded,
    then cut into strips

rind of 1 lemon, in broad strips

finely chopped fresh flat-leaf
    parsley, to garnish

method

1 Heat 1 tablespoon of the oil in a flameproof casserole over a medium–high heat. Very lightly dust one side of each cod fillet with the flour, seasoned with salt and pepper.

2 Pan-fry, floured-side down, for 2 minutes, or until just golden. Set aside. Wipe out the casserole, then heat the remaining oil over a medium–high heat. Add the onion and sauté for 5 minutes, or until soft but not browned.

3 Stir in the tomatoes, garlic, wine, paprika, salt and pepper and bring to the boil. Reduce the heat and simmer for 5 minutes, stirring occasionally.

4 Stir the red and green peppers into the casserole with the lemon strips and bring to the boil. Lay the cod fillets on top, browned-side up, and season with salt and pepper. Cover the casserole and bake in a preheated oven, 200°C/400°F/Gas Mark 6, for 12–15 minutes, depending on the thickness of the cod, until it is cooked through and flakes easily.

5 Discard the lemon rind just before serving. Serve the cod on a bed of the vegetables and sprinkled with the chopped parsley.

cod with catalan spinach

ingredients

SERVES 4

4 cod fillets, each about
   175 g/6 oz
olive oil
salt and pepper
tomato halves and lemon
   wedges, to serve

catalan spinach

55 g/2 oz raisins
55 g/2 oz pine kernels
4 tbsp extra virgin olive oil
3 garlic cloves, crushed
500 g/1 lb 2oz baby spinach
   leaves, rinsed and
   shaken dry

method

1 Put the raisins for the Catalan spinach in a small bowl, cover with hot water and set aside to soak for 15 minutes. Drain well.

2 Meanwhile, put the pine kernels in a dry frying pan over a medium–high heat and dry-fry for 1–2 minutes, shaking frequently, until toasted and golden brown: watch closely because they burn quickly.

3 Heat the oil in a large, lidded frying pan over a medium–high heat. Add the garlic and cook for 2 minutes, or until golden but not brown. Remove with a slotted spoon and discard.

4 Add the spinach to the oil, with only the rinsing water clinging to its leaves. Cover and cook for 4–5 minutes until wilted. Uncover, stir in the drained raisins and pine kernels and continue cooking until all the liquid evaporates. Season and keep warm.

5 To cook the cod, brush the fillets lightly with oil and sprinkle with salt and pepper. Place under a preheated hot grill about 10 cm/4 inches from the heat and grill for 8–10 minutes, until the flesh is opaque and flakes easily.

6 Divide the spinach between 4 plates and place the cod fillets on top. Serve with the tomato halves and lemon wedges.

marseilles-style fish stew

ingredients

SERVES 4–6

large pinch of saffron threads

2 tbsp olive oil

1 large onion, finely chopped

1 bulb of fennel, thinly sliced,
with the feathery green
fronds reserved

2 large garlic cloves, crushed

4 tbsp pastis

1 litre/1³/₄ pints fish stock

2 large sun-ripened tomatoes,
peeled, deseeded and
diced, or 400 g/14 oz
chopped tomatoes, drained

1 tbsp tomato paste

1 bay leaf

pinch of sugar

pinch of dried chilli flakes
(optional)

salt and pepper

24 large raw prawns, peeled

1 squid, cleaned and cut
into 5-mm/¹/₄-inch rings,
tentacles reserved

900 g/2 lb fresh, skinned
and boned Mediterranean
fish, such as sea bass,
monkfish, red snapper,
halibut or haddock,
cut into large chunks

method

1 Put the saffron threads in a small dry frying pan over a high heat and toast, stirring constantly, for 1 minute, or until you can smell the aroma. Immediately tip out of the pan and set aside.

2 Heat the oil in a large flameproof casserole over a medium heat, then add the onion and fennel and sauté for 3 minutes. Add the garlic and sautée for a further 5 minutes, until the onion and fennel are soft, but not coloured.

3 Remove the casserole from the heat. Warm the pastis in a ladle or small saucepan, then ignite and pour it over the onion and fennel to flambé. When the flames die down, return the casserole to the heat and stir in the stock, tomatoes, tomato paste, bay leaf, sugar, chilli flakes, if using, salt and pepper. Slowly bring to the boil, skimming the surface if necessary, then reduce the heat to low and simmer, uncovered, for 15 minutes.

4 Add the prepared prawns and squid rings and simmer until the prawns turn pink and the squid rings are opaque. Do not overcook, or they will be tough. Use a slotted spoon to transfer to serving bowls. Add the fish chunks to the broth and simmer just until the flesh flakes easily. Transfer the seafood and broth to the serving bowls and garnish with the reserved fennel fronds.

livornese seafood stew

ingredients

SERVES 8

350 g/12 oz freshly cooked
    lobster meat
350 g/12 oz prepared squid,
    sliced into rings
1.3 kg/3 lb red snapper fillets,
    sliced thickly
900 g/2 lb cod fillet, sliced
    thickly
900 g/2 lb tilapia or monkfish
    fillets, sliced thickly
salt and pepper
150 ml/5 fl oz virgin olive oil
2 onions, chopped
1 carrot, chopped
2 celery sticks, chopped
350 ml/12 fl oz dry white wine
2 litres/3$^1/_2$ pints water
400 g/14 oz canned tomatoes
1 bay leaf
1 fresh red chilli, deseeded
1 ciabatta or baguette, cut
    into 1-cm/$^1/_2$-inch slices
4 garlic cloves, 1 halved,
    3 finely chopped
900 g/2 lb live mussels,
    scrubbed and debearded
4 fresh sage leaves

method

1 Season the lobster meat, squid and fish fillets with salt and pepper and set aside.

2 Heat 4 tablespoons of the oil in a saucepan. Cook the onions, carrot and celery over a medium heat, stirring, until just starting to colour. Add 300 ml/10 fl oz of the wine, the water, tomatoes, bay leaf and chilli. Bring to the boil, then simmer for 50 minutes. Strain the stock and set aside 1.2 litres/2 pints.

3 Place the bread slices on a baking sheet and drizzle with 2 tablespoons of the olive oil. Bake in a preheated oven, 200°C/400°F/Gas Mark 6, for about 10 minutes until crisp, then rub with one of the garlic halves and set aside.

4 Put the mussels in a saucepan, add the remaining wine, cover and cook over a high heat, shaking the pan occasionally, until the shells have opened. Discard any that remain closed. Strain, reserving the liquid.

5 Heat the remaining olive oil in a saucepan, add the sage and chopped garlic and cook for 1 minute. Add the squid and cook, stirring, for 2–3 minutes, until golden. Remove the squid.

6 Add the fish fillets and stock to the pan, bring to the boil, and simmer for 5 minutes. Put all the seafood in the pan, adding 2 tablespoons of the reserved cooking liquid. Heat through for 2 minutes. Serve immediately with the garlic toasts.

spanish swordfish stew

ingredients

SERVES 4

4 tbsp olive oil

3 shallots, chopped

2 garlic cloves, chopped

225 g/8 oz canned chopped
tomatoes

1 tbsp tomato paste

650 g/1 lb 7 oz potatoes, sliced

250 ml/9 fl oz vegetable stock

2 tbsp lemon juice

1 red pepper, deseeded and
chopped

1 orange pepper, deseeded
and chopped

20 black olives, stoned
and halved

1 kg/2 lb 4 oz swordfish
steak, skinned and cut
into bite-sized pieces

salt and pepper

fresh flat-leaf parsley sprigs
and lemon slices, to
garnish

method

1 Heat the oil in a saucepan over a low heat, add the shallots and cook, stirring frequently, for 4 minutes, or until softened. Add the garlic, tomatoes and tomato paste, cover and simmer gently for 20 minutes.

2 Meanwhile, put the potatoes in an ovenproof casserole with the stock and lemon juice. Bring to the boil, then reduce the heat and add the peppers. Cover and cook for 15 minutes.

3 Add the olives, swordfish and the tomato mixture to the potatoes. Season with salt and pepper. Stir well, then cover and simmer for 7–10 minutes, or until the swordfish is cooked to your taste.

4 Remove from the heat and garnish with parsley sprigs and lemon slices.

chargrilled sea bass with stewed artichokes

ingredients

SERVES 6

1.8 kg/4 lb baby globe
   artichokes
2¹/₂ tbsp fresh lemon juice,
   plus the cut halves of
   the lemon
150 ml/5 fl oz olive oil
10 garlic cloves, finely sliced
1 tbsp chopped fresh thyme,
   plus extra to garnish
salt and pepper
6 x 115-g/4-oz sea bass fillets
1 tbsp olive oil, for brushing
crusty bread, to serve

method

1 Peel away the tough outer leaves of each artichoke until the yellow-green heart is revealed. Slice off the pointed top at about halfway between the point and the top of the stem. Cut off the stem and pare off what is left of the dark green leaves around the bottom of the artichoke.

2 Submerge the prepared artichokes in water containing the cut halves of the lemon, to prevent discoloration. When all the artichokes have been prepared, turn them choke side down and slice thickly.

3 Heat the olive oil in a large saucepan. Add the artichoke pieces, garlic, thyme, lemon juice and seasoning, cover and cook over a low heat for 20–30 minutes, without colouring, until tender.

4 Meanwhile, preheat a ridged griddle pan or light a barbecue. Brush the sea bass fillets with the 1 tablespoon olive oil and season well. Cook on the griddle pan or over hot coals for 3–4 minutes on each side until just tender.

5 Divide the stewed artichokes between 6 plates and top each with a fish fillet. Garnish with chopped thyme and serve with crusty bread.

sea bream wrapped in vine leaves

ingredients

SERVES 4

2 sea bream, about 350 g/
  12 oz each, cleaned and
  scaled
12–16 large vine leaves
thyme leaves and half a
  barbecued lemon, to
  garnish

marinade

6 tbsp olive oil
2 tbsp white wine or dry sherry
2 garlic cloves, finely chopped
2 bay leaves, crumbled
1 tbsp fresh thyme leaves
1 tbsp snipped fresh chives
salt and pepper

method

1 Rinse the fish and pat dry with kitchen paper. Score each fish 2–3 times diagonally on each side and place in a large dish. Mix together the olive oil, white wine, garlic, bay leaves, thyme and chives in a small bowl and season with salt and pepper. Spoon the mixture over the fish, turning to coat. Cover and marinate for 1 hour.

2 If using vine leaves preserved in brine, soak them in hot water for 20 minutes, then rinse well and pat dry. If using fresh vine leaves, blanch in boiling water for 3 minutes, then refresh under cold water, drain and pat dry.

3 Drain the fish, reserving the marinade. Wrap each fish in vine leaves to enclose. Brush with the marinade. Cook on a medium barbecue for 6 minutes on each side, brushing with more marinade occasionally.

4 Serve garnished with thyme leaves and half a barbecued lemon.

grilled red snapper with garlic

ingredients

SERVES 4

2 tbsp lemon juice

4 tbsp olive oil, plus extra
for oiling

salt and pepper

4 red snapper or mullet,
scaled and gutted

2 tbsp chopped fresh herbs
such as oregano, marjoram,
flat-leaf parsley or thyme

2 garlic cloves, finely chopped

2 tbsp chopped fresh
flat-leaf parsley

lemon wedges, to garnish

method

1 Preheat the grill. Put the lemon juice, oil, salt and pepper in a bowl and whisk together. Brush the mixture inside and on both sides of the fish and sprinkle on the chopped herb of your choice. Place on an oiled grill pan.

2 Grill the fish for about 10 minutes, basting frequently and turning once, until golden brown.

3 Meanwhile, mix together the chopped garlic and chopped parsley. Sprinkle the garlic mixture on top of the cooked fish and serve hot or cold, garnished with lemon wedges.

moroccan fish tagine

ingredients

SERVES 4

2 tbsp olive oil

1 large onion, finely chopped

large pinch of saffron threads

$1/2$ tsp ground cinnamon

1 tsp ground coriander

$1/2$ tsp ground cumin

$1/2$ tsp ground turmeric

200 g/7 oz canned chopped
tomatoes

300 ml/10 fl oz fish stock

4 small red snapper, cleaned,
boned, and heads and
tails removed

50 g/1$3/4$ oz stoned green
olives

1 tbsp chopped preserved
lemon

3 tbsp chopped fresh
coriander

salt and pepper

freshly prepared couscous or
crusty bread, to serve

method

1 Heat the oil in a large saucepan or ovenproof casserole over a low heat, add the onion and cook, stirring occasionally, for 10 minutes until softened, but not browned. Add the saffron, cinnamon, coriander, cumin and turmeric and cook, stirring constantly, for a further 30 seconds.

2 Add the tomatoes and stock and stir well. Bring to the boil, then reduce the heat, cover and simmer for 15 minutes. Uncover and simmer for a further 20–35 minutes until thickened.

3 Cut each snapper in half, then add the pieces to the pan, pushing them into the sauce. Simmer gently for a further 5–6 minutes until the fish is just cooked.

4 Carefully stir in the olives, preserved lemon and coriander. Season with salt and pepper and serve with couscous or crusty bread.

red snapper with capers & olives

ingredients

SERVES 4

700 g/1 lb 9 oz red snapper fillets (about 12)

3 tbsp chopped fresh marjoram or flat-leaf parsley

salt and pepper

thinly peeled rind of 1 orange, cut into thin strips

225 g/8 oz mixed salad leaves, torn into pieces

175 ml/6 fl oz extra virgin olive oil

1 tbsp balsamic vinegar

1 tbsp white wine vinegar

1 tsp Dijon mustard

3 tbsp virgin olive oil

1 fennel bulb, cut into thin sticks

sauce

1 tbsp butter

40 g/1 1/2 oz black olives, stoned and thinly sliced

1 tbsp capers, rinsed

method

1 Place the fish fillets on a large plate, sprinkle with the marjoram and season with salt and pepper. Set aside.

2 Blanch the orange rind in a small saucepan of boiling water for 2 minutes, drain, refresh under cold water and drain well again.

3 Place the mixed salad leaves in a large bowl. Whisk together the extra virgin olive oil, balsamic vinegar, wine vinegar and mustard in a small bowl and season. Pour the dressing over the salad leaves and toss well. Arrange on a large serving platter.

4 Heat the virgin olive oil in a heavy-based frying pan. Add the fennel and cook, stirring constantly, for 1 minute. Remove the fennel with a slotted spoon, set aside and keep warm. Add the fish fillets, skin-side down, and cook for 2 minutes. Carefully turn them over and cook for a further 1–2 minutes. Remove from the frying pan and drain on kitchen paper. Keep warm.

5 To make the sauce, melt the butter in a small saucepan, add the olives and capers and cook, stirring constantly, for 1 minute.

6 Place the fish fillets on the bed of salad leaves, top with the orange rind and fennel and pour over the sauce. Serve immediately.

sicilian tuna

ingredients

SERVES 4

marinade

125 ml/4 fl oz extra virgin
    olive oil
4 garlic cloves, finely chopped
4 fresh red chillies, deseeded
    and finely chopped
juice and finely grated rind
    of 2 lemons
4 tbsp finely chopped fresh
    flat-leaf parsley
salt and pepper

4 x 150-g/5-oz tuna steaks
2 fennel bulbs, thickly sliced
    lengthways
2 red onions, sliced
2 tbsp virgin olive oil
rocket salad and crusty
    bread, to serve

method

1 First, make the marinade by whisking all the ingredients together in a bowl. Place the tuna steaks in a large shallow dish and spoon over 4 tablespoons of the marinade, turning to coat. Cover and set aside for 30 minutes. Set aside the remaining marinade.

2 Heat a ridged griddle pan. Put the fennel and onions in a bowl, add the oil and toss well to coat. Add to the griddle pan and cook for 5 minutes on each side, until just starting to colour. Transfer to 4 warmed serving plates, drizzle with the reserved marinade, and keep warm.

3 Add the tuna steaks to the griddle pan and cook, turning once, for 4–5 minutes, until firm to the touch but still moist inside. Transfer the tuna to the plates and serve immediately with the rocket salad and crusty bread.

salad niçoise

ingredients

SERVES 4–6

2 tuna steaks, about 2 cm/
    ³/₄ inch thick

olive oil

salt and pepper

250 g/9 oz French beans,
    trimmed

2 hearts of lettuce, leaves
    separated

3 large hard-boiled eggs,
    cut into quarters

2 juicy vine-ripened tomatoes,
    cut into wedges

50 g/1³/₄ oz anchovy fillets
    in oil, drained

55 g/2 oz black olives

torn fresh basil leaves,
    to garnish

garlic vinaigrette

125 ml/4 fl oz olive or other
    vegetable oil

3 tbsp white wine vinegar or
    lemon juice

1 tsp Dijon mustard

¹/₂ tsp caster sugar

salt and pepper

method

1 To make the garlic vinaigrette, put all the ingredients in a screw-top jar, secure the lid and shake well until an emulsion forms. Taste and adjust the seasoning if necessary.

2 Heat a ridged griddle pan over a high heat until you can feel the heat rising from the surface. Brush the tuna steaks with oil, then place, oiled-side down, on the hot pan and chargrill for 2 minutes.

3 Lightly brush the top side of the tuna steaks with a little more oil. Use a pair of tongs to turn the tuna steaks over, then season to taste. Continue chargilling for a further 2 minutes for rare or up to 4 minutes for well done. Let cool.

4 Meanwhile, bring a saucepan of salted water to the boil. Add the beans and return to the boil, then boil for 3 minutes, or until tender-crisp. Drain the beans and immediately transfer them to a large bowl. Pour over the garlic vinaigrette and stir together, then set aside to cool.

5 To serve, line a platter with lettuce leaves. Lift the beans out of the bowl, leaving the excess dressing behind, and pile them in the centre of the platter. Break the tuna into large flakes and arrange it over the beans.

6 Put the hard-boiled eggs and tomatoes around the edge and arrange the anchovy fillets, olives and basil on the salad. Drizzle over the remaining dressing and serve.

grilled tuna & vegetable kebabs

ingredients

SERVES 4

4 tuna steaks, about 140 g/
    5 oz each

2 red onions

12 cherry tomatoes

1 red pepper, deseeded and
    diced into 2.5-cm/1-inch
    pieces

1 yellow pepper, deseeded
    and diced into 2.5-cm/
    1-inch pieces

1 courgette, sliced

1 tbsp chopped fresh oregano

4 tbsp olive oil

pepper

lime wedges, to garnish

method

1 Preheat the grill to high. Cut the tuna into 2.5-cm/1-inch dice. Peel the onions, leaving the root intact, and cut each onion lengthways into 6 wedges.

2 Divide the fish, onions, tomatoes, peppers and courgettes evenly between 8 wooden skewers (presoaked to avoid burning) and arrange on the grill pan.

3 Mix the oregano and oil together in a small bowl. Season with pepper. Lightly brush the kebabs with the oil and cook under a grill preheated to high for 10–15 minutes or until evenly cooked, turning occasionally. If you cannot fit all the kebabs on the grill pan at once, cook them in batches, keeping the cooked kebabs warm while cooking the remainder. Alternatively, these kebabs can be cooked on a barbecue.

4 Garnish with lime wedges.

fresh sardines baked with lemon & oregano

ingredients

SERVES 4

2 lemons, plus extra lemon
	wedges, to garnish
12 large fresh sardines, cleaned
4 tbsp olive oil
4 tbsp chopped fresh oregano
salt and pepper

method

1 Slice one of the lemons and grate the rind and squeeze the juice from the second lemon.

2 Cut the heads off the sardines. Put the fish in a shallow, ovenproof dish large enough to hold them in a single layer. Put the lemon slices between the fish. Drizzle the lemon juice and oil over the fish. Sprinkle over the lemon rind and oregano and season with salt and pepper.

3 Bake in a preheated oven, 190°C/375°F/Gas Mark 5, for 20–30 minutes until the fish are tender. Serve garnished with lemon wedges.

north african sardines

ingredients

SERVES 4

500 g/1 lb 2 oz fresh sardines,
   cleaned and scaled
barbecued lemon halves,
   to garnish

marinade

6 tbsp olive oil

3 tbsp lemon juice

3 tbsp chopped fresh
   coriander

2 tsp finely grated lemon rind

$1/2$ tsp ground cumin

$1/4$ tsp paprika

salt and pepper

method

1 Place the sardines in a large, shallow dish. Mix together the olive oil, lemon juice, coriander, lemon rind, cumin and paprika in a bowl and season with salt and pepper. Pour the mixture over the fish, turning to coat. Cover and stand in a cool place to marinate for 1 hour.

2 Drain the fish, reserving the marinade. Place the sardines in a wire barbecue basket.

3 Cook on a medium barbecue, brushing frequently with the marinade, for about 3 minutes on each side, or until browned. Serve immediately, garnished with barbecued lemon halves.

lemon-marinated prawns with mint pesto

ingredients

SERVES 4

750 g/1 lb 10 oz raw jumbo
   prawns
juice of 2 lemons
1 bunch fresh mint, chopped
2 garlic cloves, very finely
   chopped

mint pesto

1 garlic clove, roughly chopped
8 tbsp fresh mint, roughly
   chopped
3 tbsp extra virgin olive oil
1 tbsp red wine vinegar
1 tbsp soured cream or
   double cream
1 tbsp grated Parmesan
   cheese
salt and pepper

method

1 Shell and devein the prawns. Place them in a shallow dish and sprinkle with the lemon juice, mint and garlic. Toss well to coat, cover and marinate for 30 minutes.

2 To make the pesto, put all the ingredients in a blender or food processor and process until smooth. Scrape into a bowl, then cover and chill until required.

3 Drain the prawns and thread them onto skewers (presoaked if using wooden ones). Cook on a medium barbecue for 2–3 minutes on each side, or until they have turned pink and are cooked through.

4 Remove the prawns from the skewers and transfer to serving plates. Add a spoonful of mint pesto and serve.

prawn pilau

ingredients

SERVES 4

3 tbsp olive oil

1 onion, finely chopped

1 red pepper, cored,
   deseeded and thinly sliced

1 garlic clove, crushed

225 g/8 oz long-grain white
   rice

750 ml/generous 1¼ pints
   fish, chicken or vegetable
   stock

1 bay leaf

salt and pepper

400 g/14 oz peeled cooked
   prawns, thawed and
   drained if frozen

grated kefalotiri or romano
   cheese and cubes of feta
   cheese, to serve

to garnish

whole cooked prawns

lemon wedges

black Greek olives

method

1 Heat the oil in a large, lidded frying pan, add the onion, red pepper and garlic, and fry for 5 minutes, until softened. Add the rice and cook for 2–3 minutes, stirring all the time, until the grains look transparent.

2 Add the stock, bay leaf, salt and pepper. Bring to the boil, cover the pan with a tightly fitting lid, and simmer for about 15 minutes, until the rice is tender and the liquid has been absorbed. Do not stir during cooking. When cooked, very gently stir in the prawns.

3 Remove the lid, cover the frying pan with a clean tea towel, replace the lid and stand in a warm place for 10 minutes to dry out. Stir with a fork to separate the grains.

4 Serve garnished with whole prawns, lemon wedges and black olives. Accompany with grated kefalotiri or romano cheese, for sprinkling on top, and a bowl of feta cubes.

seafood paella
with lemon & herbs

ingredients

SERVES 4–6

$1/2$ tsp saffron threads

2 tbsp hot water

150 g/$5^1/2$ oz cod fillet, skinned
and rinsed under cold
running water

1.3 litres/$2^1/4$ pints simmering
fish stock

12 large raw prawns, peeled
and deveined

450 g/1 lb raw squid, cleaned
and cut into rings or
bite-sized pieces
(or use the same quantity
of shucked scallops)

3 tbsp olive oil

1 large red onion, chopped

2 garlic cloves, crushed

1 small fresh red chilli,
deseeded and minced

225 g/8 oz tomatoes, peeled
and cut into wedges

375 g/13 oz medium-grain
paella rice

1 tbsp chopped fresh parsley

2 tsp chopped fresh dill

salt and pepper

1 lemon, cut into halves,
to serve

method

1 Put the saffron threads and water in a small bowl for a few minutes to infuse.

2 Add the cod to the saucepan of simmering stock and cook for 5 minutes, then transfer to a colander, rinse under cold running water and drain. Add the prawns and squid to the stock and cook for 2 minutes. Cut the cod into chunks, then transfer, with the other seafood, to a bowl and set aside. Let the stock simmer.

3 Heat the oil in a paella pan and stir the onion over a medium heat until softened. Add the garlic, chilli and saffron and its soaking liquid and cook, stirring, for 1 minute. Add the tomato wedges and cook, stirring, for 2 minutes. Add the rice and herbs and cook, stirring, for 1 minute. Add most of the stock and bring to the boil. Simmer, uncovered, for 10 minutes. Do not stir during cooking, but shake the pan once or twice, and when adding ingredients. Season and cook for 10 minutes, until the rice is almost cooked. Add more stock if necessary. Add the seafood and cook for 2 minutes.

4 When all the liquid has been absorbed and you detect a faint toasty aroma coming from the rice, remove from the heat immediately. Cover with foil and let stand for 5 minutes.

paella with mussels & white wine

ingredients

SERVES 4–6

150 g/5^1/$_2$ oz cod fillet, skinned
and rinsed in cold water

1.3 litres/2^1/$_4$ pints simmering
fish stock

200 g/7 oz live mussels,
scrubbed and debearded

3 tbsp olive oil

1 large red onion, chopped

2 garlic cloves, crushed

^{1}/$_2$ tsp cayenne pepper

^{1}/$_2$ tsp saffron threads infused
in 2 tbsp hot water

225 g/8 oz tomatoes, peeled
and cut into wedges

1 red pepper, deseeded
and sliced

1 green pepper, deseeded
and sliced

375 g/13 oz medium-grain
paella rice

100 ml/3^1/$_2$ fl oz white wine

150 g/5^1/$_2$ oz shelled peas

1 tbsp chopped fresh dill,
plus extra to garnish

salt and pepper

lemon wedges, to serve

method

1 Cook the cod in the saucepan of simmering stock for 5 minutes. Transfer to a colander, rinse under cold running water and drain. Cut into chunks, then transfer to a bowl. Cook the mussels in the stock for 5 minutes, or until opened. Discard any that remain closed, then transfer to the bowl with the cod and set aside.

2 Heat the oil in a paella pan and stir the onion over a medium heat until softened. Add the garlic, cayenne pepper and saffron and its soaking liquid and cook, stirring constantly, for 1 minute. Add the tomatoes and peppers and cook, stirring, for 2 minutes.

3 Add the rice and cook, stirring, for 1 minute. Add the wine and most of the stock and bring to the boil, then simmer for 10 minutes. Do not stir during cooking, but shake the pan once or twice, and when adding ingredients. Add the peas and dill and season. Cook for 10 minutes, or until the rice is almost cooked, adding more stock if necessary. Add the cod and mussels and cook for 3 minutes.

4 When all the liquid has been absorbed and you detect a faint toasty aroma coming from the rice, remove from the heat immediately. Cover with foil and let stand for 5 minutes. Garnish with dill and serve with lemon wedges.

seafood risotto

ingredients

SERVES 4

225 g/8 oz prepared raw
  prawns, heads and
  shells reserved
2 garlic cloves, halved
1 lemon, sliced
225 g/8 oz live mussels,
  scrubbed and debearded
225 g/8 oz live clams,
  scrubbed
600 ml/1 pint water
115 g/4 oz butter
1 tbsp olive oil
1 onion, finely chopped
2 tbsp chopped fresh
  flat-leaf parsley
350 g/12 oz arborio rice
125 ml/4 fl oz dry white wine
225 g/8 oz cleaned raw squid,
  cut into small pieces, or
  squid rings
4 tbsp Marsala
salt and pepper

method

1 Wrap the prawn heads and shells in a square of muslin and pound with a pestle. Put the wrapped shells and their liquid in a saucepan with the garlic, lemon, mussels and clams. Add the water, cover and bring to the boil over a high heat. Cook, shaking the pan frequently, for 5 minutes until the shellfish have opened. Discard any that remain closed. Cool, then shell and set aside. Strain the cooking liquid through a muslin-lined sieve and add water to make 1.2 litres/2 pints. Bring to the boil in a saucepan, then simmer over a low heat.

2 Melt 2 tablespoons of butter with the olive oil in a saucepan. Cook the onion and half the parsley over a medium heat, stirring often, until softened. Reduce the heat, stir in the rice and cook, stirring, until the grains are translucent. Add the wine and cook, stirring, for 1 minute. Add the hot cooking liquid a ladleful at a time, stirring constantly, until all the liquid is absorbed and the rice is creamy.

3 Melt 55 g/2 oz of the butter in a pan. Cook the squid, stirring frequently, for 3 minutes. Add the prawns and cook for 2–3 minutes, until the squid is opaque and the prawns have changed colour. Add the Marsala, bring to the boil and cook until the liquid has evaporated. Stir all the seafood into the rice, add the remaining butter and parsley, and season. Heat gently and serve immediately.

vegetarian

Brightly coloured vegetables and taste-bud-tingling flavours such as olive oil, garlic, citrus fruits and herbs feature prominently in the Mediterranean diet, so although the various countries are not specifically vegetarian-friendly, there are plenty of dishes to keep a vegetarian happy! Choose one of the hearty main dishes, such as Aubergine Tagine with Polenta, Roasted Vegetable Moussaka, Courgette & Cheese Gratin, Artichoke Paella, Spinach & Feta Pie or Spanish Tortilla, and surround it with some of the wonderful side dishes – Oven-dried Tomatoes, Crispy Roasted Fennel, Parmesan Pumpkin, Spinach with Chickpeas and a Roasted Pepper Salad – for a satisfying and very appetizing vegetarian feast.

These dishes also make great accompaniments to meat or fish dishes, or can be served as part of an alfresco summer lunch or evening party. Roasted Summer Vegetables, Stuffed Courgettes with Walnuts & Feta, Roasted Red Peppers with Halloumi, Toasted Pine Kernel & Vegetable Couscous, Greek Salad and Tabbouleh will all look wonderful served in colourful bowls and arranged on a generously sized table covered in a cheerful cloth. The food will taste absolutely delicious and will certainly be a great talking point for your guests!

aubergine tagine with polenta

ingredients

SERVES 4

1 aubergine, cut into
   1-cm/^{1}/$_2$-inch cubes
3 tbsp olive oil
1 large onion, thinly sliced
1 carrot, diced
2 garlic cloves, chopped
115 g/4 oz mushrooms, sliced
2 tsp ground coriander
2 tsp cumin seeds
1 tsp chilli powder
1 tsp ground turmeric
600 ml/1 pint canned
   chopped tomatoes
300 ml/10 fl oz vegetable
   stock
1 tbsp tomato paste
75 g/2^3/$_4$ oz ready-to-eat dried
   apricots, roughly chopped
400 g/14 oz canned
   chickpeas, drained
2 tbsp fresh coriander,
   to garnish

polenta

1.2 litres/2 pints hot vegetable
   stock
200 g/7 oz instant polenta

method

1 Toss the aubergine in 1 tablespoon of the oil and arrange in a grill pan. Cook under a grill preheated to medium for 20 minutes, turning occasionally, until softened and starting to blacken around the edges – brush with more oil if the aubergine becomes too dry.

2 Heat the remaining oil in a large, heavy-based saucepan over a medium heat. Add the onion and cook, stirring occasionally, for 8 minutes, or until soft and golden. Add the carrot, garlic and mushrooms and cook for 5 minutes. Add the spices and cook, stirring constantly, for a further minute.

3 Add the tomatoes and stock, stir well, then add the tomato paste. Bring to the boil, then reduce the heat and simmer for 10 minutes, or until the sauce starts to thicken and reduce. Add the aubergine, apricots and chickpeas, partially cover, and cook for a further 10 minutes, stirring occasionally.

4 Meanwhile, to make the polenta, pour the hot stock into a saucepan and bring to the boil. Pour in the polenta in a steady stream, stirring constantly with a wooden spoon. Reduce the heat to low and cook for 1–2 minutes, or until the polenta thickens. Serve the tagine with the polenta, sprinkled with the fresh coriander.

roasted vegetable moussaka

ingredients

SERVES 4–6

1 large aubergine, thickly
    sliced

2 medium courgettes, thickly
    sliced

2 onions, cut into small
    wedges

2 red peppers, cored,
    deseeded and roughly
    chopped

2 garlic cloves, peeled and
    roughly chopped

5 tbsp olive oil

1 tbsp chopped fresh thyme

salt and pepper

2 eggs, beaten

300 ml/10 fl oz Greek-style
    yogurt

400 g/14 oz canned chopped
    tomatoes in juice

55 g/2 oz feta cheese

method

1 Put the aubergine, courgettes, onions, peppers and garlic in a roasting tin. Drizzle over the oil, toss together, and then sprinkle over the thyme and season with salt and pepper. Roast in a preheated oven, 220°C/425°F/Gas Mark 7, for 30–35 minutes, turning the tin halfway through the cooking, until golden brown and tender.

2 Meanwhile, beat together the eggs and yogurt and season with salt and pepper. When the vegetables are cooked, reduce the oven temperature to 180°C/350°F/Gas Mark 4.

3 Put half the vegetables in a layer in a large ovenproof dish. Spoon over the canned chopped tomatoes and their juice, then add the remaining vegetables. Pour over the yogurt mixture and crumble over the feta cheese. Bake in the oven for 45 minutes to 1 hour, until golden brown. Serve hot, warm or cold.

roasted summer vegetables

ingredients

SERVES 4

2 tbsp olive oil

1 fennel bulb

2 red onions

2 beefsteak tomatoes

1 aubergine

2 courgettes

1 yellow pepper

1 red pepper

1 orange pepper

4 garlic cloves, peeled but
   left whole

4 fresh rosemary sprigs

pepper

crusty bread, to serve (optional)

method

1 Brush a large ovenproof dish with a little of the oil. Prepare the vegetables. Cut the fennel bulb, red onions, and tomatoes into wedges. Slice the aubergine and courgettes thickly, then deseed all the peppers and cut into chunks. Arrange the vegetables in the dish and tuck the garlic cloves and rosemary sprigs among them. Drizzle with the remaining oil and season with pepper.

2 Roast the vegetables in a preheated oven, 200°C/400°F/Gas Mark 6, for 10 minutes. Remove the dish from the oven and turn the vegetables over using a slotted spoon. Return the dish to the oven and roast for a further 10–15 minutes, or until the vegetables are tender and starting to turn golden brown.

3 Serve the vegetables straight from the dish or transfer them to a warmed serving plate. For a vegetarian main course, serve with crusty bread, if you like.

rustic roasted ratatouille

ingredients

SERVES 4

300 g/10^1/$_2$ oz potatoes in their skins, scrubbed

200 g/7 oz aubergine, cut into 1-cm/^{1}/$_2$-inch wedges

125 g/4^1/$_2$ oz red onion cut into 5-mm/^{1}/$_4$-inch slices

200 g/7 oz mixed peppers, deseeded and sliced into 1-cm/^{1}/$_2$-inch strips

175 g/6 oz courgette, cut in half lengthways, then into 1-cm/^{1}/$_2$-inch slices

125 g/4^1/$_2$ oz cherry tomatoes

90 g/3^1/$_4$ oz fromage frais

1 tsp runny honey

pinch of smoked paprika

1 tsp chopped fresh parsley, to garnish

marinade

1 tsp vegetable oil

1 tbsp lemon juice

4 tbsp white wine

1 tsp sugar

2 tbsp chopped fresh basil

1 tsp finely chopped fresh rosemary

1 tbsp finely chopped fresh lemon thyme

^{1}/$_4$ tsp smoked paprika

method

1 Bake the potatoes in a preheated oven, 200°C/400°F/Gas Mark 6, for 30 minutes, then remove and cut into wedges – the flesh should not be completely cooked.

2 To make the marinade, place all the ingredients in a bowl and blend with a hand-held electric blender until smooth, or use a food processor.

3 Put the potato wedges into a large bowl with the aubergine, onion, peppers and courgette, then pour over the marinade and mix thoroughly.

4 Arrange on a non-stick baking tray and roast in the oven, turning occasionally, for 25–30 minutes, or until golden brown and tender. Add the tomatoes for the last 5 minutes of the cooking time, just to split the skins and warm slightly.

5 Mix the fromage frais, honey and paprika together in a bowl.

6 Serve the vegetables with the fromage frais mixture, and sprinkle with chopped parsley, to garnish.

stuffed courgettes with walnuts & feta

ingredients

SERVES 4

4 fat, medium courgettes

3 tbsp olive oil

1 onion, finely chopped

1 garlic clove, finely chopped

55 g/2 oz feta cheese,
     crumbled

25 g/1 oz walnut pieces,
     chopped

55 g/2 oz white breadcrumbs

1 egg, beaten

1 tsp chopped fresh dill

salt and pepper

method

1 Put the courgettes in a saucepan of boiling water, return to the boil, then boil for 3 minutes. Drain, rinse under cold water and drain again. Let cool.

2 When the courgettes are cool enough to handle, cut a thin strip off the top side of each one with a sharp knife. Using a teaspoon, carefully scoop out the flesh, leaving a shell to hold the stuffing. Chop the courgette flesh.

3 Heat 2 tablespoons of the oil in a saucepan. Add the onion and garlic and fry for 5 minutes, until softened. Add the courgette flesh and fry for 5 minutes, until the onion is golden brown. Remove from the heat and cool slightly. Stir in the cheese then the walnuts, breadcrumbs, egg, dill, salt and pepper.

4 Use the stuffing to fill the courgette shells, and place side by side in an ovenproof dish. Drizzle over the remaining oil.

5 Cover the dish with foil and bake in a preheated oven, 190°C/375°F/Gas Mark 5, for 30 minutes. Remove the foil and bake for another 10–15 minutes or until golden brown. Serve hot.

courgette & cheese gratin

ingredients

SERVES 4–6

55 g/2 oz unsalted butter,
   plus extra for greasing
6 courgettes, sliced
salt and pepper
2 tbsp chopped fresh
   tarragon or a mixture of
   mint, tarragon and
   flat-leaf parsley
200 g/7 oz Gruyère or
   Parmesan cheese, grated
125 ml/4 fl oz milk
125 ml/4 fl oz double cream
2 eggs
freshly grated nutmeg

method

1 Melt the butter in a large sauté pan or frying pan over a medium–high heat. Add the courgettes and sauté for 4–6 minutes, turning the slices over occasionally, until coloured on both sides. Remove from the pan and drain on kitchen paper, then season with salt and pepper.

2 Spread half the courgettes over the bottom of a greased ovenproof serving dish. Sprinkle with half the herbs and 55 g/2 oz of the cheese. Repeat these layers once more.

3 Mix the milk, cream and eggs together and season with nutmeg, salt and pepper. Pour this liquid over the courgettes, then sprinkle the top with the remaining cheese.

4 Bake the gratin in a preheated oven, 350°F/180°C, for 35–45 minutes, or until it is set in the centre and golden brown. Remove from the oven and let stand for 5 minutes before serving straight from the dish.

paella de verduras

ingredients

SERVES 4–6

$^1/_2$ tsp saffron threads

2 tbsp hot water

3 tbsp olive oil

1 large onion, chopped

2 garlic cloves, crushed

1 tsp paprika

225 g/8 oz tomatoes, peeled
and cut into wedges

1 red pepper, halved and
deseeded, then grilled,
peeled and sliced

1 green pepper, halved and
deseeded, then grilled,
peeled and sliced

425 g/15 oz canned
chickpeas, drained

350 g/12 oz medium-grain
paella rice

1.3 litres/2$^1/_4$ pints simmering
vegetable stock

55 g/2 oz shelled peas

150 g/5$^1/_2$ oz fresh asparagus
spears, blanched

1 tbsp chopped fresh flat-leaf
parsley, plus extra
to garnish

salt and pepper

1 lemon, cut into wedges,
to serve

method

1 Put the saffron threads and water in a small bowl to infuse for a few minutes.

2 Meanwhile, heat the oil in a paella pan and cook the onion over a medium heat, stirring, for 2–3 minutes, or until softened. Add the garlic, paprika and saffron and its soaking liquid and cook, stirring, for 1 minute. Add the tomatoes, peppers and chickpeas and cook, stirring, for a further 2 minutes.

3 Add the rice and cook, stirring constantly, for 1 minute, or until glossy and coated. Pour in most of the hot stock and bring to the boil. Reduce the heat and simmer, uncovered, for 10 minutes. Do not stir during cooking, but shake the pan once or twice. Add the peas, asparagus and parsley and season with salt and pepper. Shake the pan and cook for a further 10–15 minutes, or until the rice grains are plump and cooked. Pour in a little more hot stock if necessary, then shake the pan to spread the liquid through the paella.

4 When all the liquid has been absorbed and you detect a faint toasty aroma coming from the rice, remove from the heat immediately to prevent burning. Cover the pan with foil and let stand for 5 minutes. Sprinkle over chopped parsley to garnish and serve direct from the pan, with the lemon wedges for squeezing over the rice.

artichoke paella

ingredients

SERVES 4–6

$1/2$ tsp saffron threads

2 tbsp hot water

3 tbsp olive oil

1 large onion, chopped

1 courgette, roughly chopped

2 garlic cloves, crushed

$1/4$ tsp cayenne pepper

225 g/8 oz tomatoes, peeled
    and cut into wedges

425 g/15 oz canned
    chickpeas, drained

425 g/15 oz canned
    artichokes hearts, drained
    and roughly sliced

350 g/12 oz medium-grain
    paella rice

1.3 litres/$2^1/4$ pints simmering
    vegetable stock

150 g/$5^1/2$ oz French beans,
    blanched

salt and pepper

1 lemon, cut into wedges,
    to serve

method

1 Put the saffron threads and water in a small bowl to infuse for a few minutes.

2 Meanwhile, heat the oil in a paella pan and cook the onion and courgette over a medium heat, stirring, for 2–3 minutes, or until softened. Add the garlic, cayenne pepper, and saffron and its soaking liquid and cook, stirring constantly, for 1 minute. Add the tomato wedges, chickpeas and artichokes and cook, stirring, for a further 2 minutes.

3 Add the rice and cook, stirring constantly, for 1 minute, or until the rice is glossy and coated. Pour in most of the hot stock and bring to the boil, then simmer, uncovered, for 10 minutes. Do not stir during cooking, but shake the pan once or twice. Add the French beans and season. Shake the pan and cook for a further 10–15 minutes, or until the rice grains are plump and cooked. If the liquid is absorbed too quickly, pour in a little more hot stock, then shake the pan to spread the liquid through the paella.

4 When all the liquid has been absorbed and you detect a faint toasty aroma coming from the rice, remove from the heat immediately to prevent burning. Cover the pan with foil and let stand for 5 minutes. Serve direct from the pan with the lemon wedges to squeeze over the rice.

roasted red peppers with halloumi

ingredients

SERVES 6

6 small red peppers

2 tbsp olive oil, plus extra
for oiling

3 garlic cloves, thinly sliced

250 g/9 oz halloumi or feta
cheese, thinly sliced

12 fresh mint leaves

grated rind and juice of
1 lemon

1 tbsp chopped fresh thyme

3 tbsp pine kernels

pepper

method

1 Cut the peppers in half lengthways and remove the cores and seeds. Rub the skins of the peppers with a little of the oil, then arrange the peppers, skin-side down, on a large oiled baking sheet.

2 Scatter half the garlic into the peppers. Add the cheese, then the mint leaves, lemon rind, remaining garlic, thyme, pine kernels and pepper. Drizzle over the remaining oil and the lemon juice.

3 Roast the peppers in a preheated oven, 200°C/400°F/Gas Mark 6, for 30 minutes, until tender and beginning to char around the edges. Serve warm.

oven-dried tomatoes

ingredients

SERVES 4

1 kg/2 lb 4 oz large, juicy full-
 flavoured tomatoes
sea salt
500 g/1 lb 2 oz buffalo
 mozzarella, sliced
extra virgin olive oil, for
 drizzling
pepper
basil leaves, to garnish

method

1 Using a sharp knife, cut each of the tomatoes into quarters lengthways. Using a teaspoon, scoop out the seeds and discard. If the tomatoes are large, cut each quarter in half lengthways again.

2 Sprinkle sea salt in a roasting tin and arrange the tomato slices, skin side down, on top. Roast in a preheated oven, 120°C/250°F/ Gas Mark 1/2, for 2 1/2 hours, or until the edges are just beginning to look charred and the flesh is dry but still pliable. The exact roasting time and yield will depend on the size and juiciness of the tomatoes. Check the tomatoes at 30-minute intervals after 1 1/2 hours.

3 Remove the dried tomatoes from the roasting tin and let cool completely. Serve with slices of buffalo mozzarella, drizzled with olive oil and sprinkled with pepper and basil leaves.

toasted pine kernel & vegetable couscous

ingredients

SERVES 4

115 g/4 oz dried green lentils

55 g/2 oz pine kernels

1 tbsp olive oil

1 onion, diced

2 garlic cloves, crushed

280 g/10 oz courgettes, sliced

250 g/9 oz tomatoes, chopped

400 g/14 oz canned artichoke
hearts, drained and cut in
half lengthways

250 g/9 oz couscous

500 ml/18 fl oz vegetable
stock

3 tbsp torn fresh basil leaves,
plus extra leaves to garnish

pepper

method

1 Put the lentils into a saucepan with plenty of cold water, bring to the boil, and boil rapidly for 10 minutes. Reduce the heat, cover and simmer for 15 minutes, or until tender.

2 Meanwhile, preheat the grill to medium. Spread the pine kernels out in a single layer on a baking sheet and toast under the preheated grill, turning to brown evenly – watch constantly because they brown quickly. Tip the pine kernels into a small dish and set aside.

3 Heat the oil in a frying pan over a medium heat, add the onion, garlic and courgettes and cook, stirring frequently, for 8–10 minutes, or until tender and the courgettes have browned slightly. Add the tomatoes and artichoke halves and heat through thoroughly for 5 minutes.

4 Meanwhile, put the couscous into a heatproof bowl. Bring the stock to the boil in a saucepan and pour over the couscous, cover and let stand for 10 minutes until the couscous absorbs the stock and becomes tender.

5 Drain the lentils and stir into the couscous. Stir in the torn basil leaves and season well with pepper. Transfer the couscous to a warmed serving dish and spoon over the cooked vegetables. Sprinkle the pine kernels over the top, garnish with basil leaves and serve immediately.

parmesan pumpkin

ingredients

SERVES 6

2 tbsp virgin olive oil

1 onion, finely chopped

1 garlic clove, finely chopped

400 ml/14 fl oz strained
  tomatoes

10 fresh basil leaves,
  shredded

2 tbsp chopped fresh
  flat-leaf parsley

1 tsp sugar

salt and pepper

2 eggs, lightly beaten

55 g/2 oz dried white
  breadcrumbs

1.6 kg/3 lb 8 oz pumpkin,
  peeled, deseeded and
  sliced

55 g/2 oz butter, plus extra
  for greasing

55 g/2 oz freshly grated
  Parmesan cheese

method

1 Heat the olive oil in a large saucepan, add the onion and garlic and cook over a low heat for 5 minutes, until softened. Stir in the strained tomatoes, basil, parsley and sugar, and season with salt and pepper. Simmer for 10–15 minutes, until thickened.

2 Meanwhile, put the beaten eggs in a shallow dish and spread out the breadcrumbs in another shallow dish. Dip the slices of pumpkin first in the egg, then in the breadcrumbs to coat, shaking off any excess.

3 Grease a large ovenproof dish with butter. Melt the butter in a large, heavy-based frying pan. Add the pumpkin slices, in batches, and cook until browned all over. Transfer the slices to the dish. Pour the sauce over them and sprinkle with the Parmesan.

4 Bake in a preheated oven, 180°C/350°F/ Gas Mark 4, for 30 minutes, until the cheese is bubbling and golden. Serve immediately.

crispy roasted fennel

ingredients

SERVES 4–6

3 large fennel bulbs

4 tbsp olive oil

finely grated rind and juice of
   1 small lemon

1 garlic clove, finely chopped

55 g/2 oz fresh white
   breadcrumbs

salt and pepper

method

1 Trim the fennel bulbs, reserving the green feathery fronds, and cut into quarters. Cook the bulbs in a large saucepan of boiling salted water for 5 minutes until just tender, then drain well.

2 Heat 2 tablespoons of the olive oil in a small roasting tin or frying pan with an ovenproof handle, then add the fennel and turn to coat in the oil. Drizzle over the lemon juice. Roast the fennel in a preheated oven, 200°C/400°F/Gas Mark 6, for about 35 minutes, until beginning to brown.

3 Meanwhile, heat the remaining oil in a frying pan. Add the garlic and fry for 1 minute, until lightly browned. Add the breadcrumbs and fry for about 5 minutes, stirring frequently, until crisp. Remove from the heat and stir in the lemon rind, reserved snipped fennel fronds, salt and pepper.

4 When the fennel is cooked, sprinkle the breadcrumb mixture over the top and return to the oven for another 5 minutes. Serve hot.

spinach with chickpeas

ingredients

SERVES 4–6

2 tbsp olive oil

1 large garlic clove, cut in half

1 medium onion,
    finely chopped

$1/2$ tsp cumin

pinch cayenne pepper

pinch turmeric

800 g/1 lb 12 oz canned
    chickpeas, drained
    and rinsed

500 g/1 lb 2 oz baby spinach
    leaves, rinsed and
    shaken dry

2 pimientos del piquillo,
    drained and sliced

salt and pepper

method

1 Heat the oil in a large, lidded frying pan over a medium–high heat. Add the garlic and cook for 2 minutes, or until golden but not brown. Remove the garlic with a slotted spoon and discard.

2 Add the onion and cumin, cayenne and turmeric and cook, stirring, for about 5 minutes until soft. Add the chickpeas and stir around until they are lightly coloured with the turmeric and cayenne.

3 Stir in the spinach with just the water clinging to its leaves. Cover and cook for 4–5 minutes until wilted. Uncover, stir in the pimientos del piquillo and continue cooking, stirring gently, until all the liquid evaporates. Season with salt and pepper and serve.

spinach & feta pie

ingredients

SERVES 6

2 tbsp olive oil

1 large onion, finely chopped

1 kg/2 lb 4 oz fresh young
   spinach leaves, washed or
   500 g/1 lb 2 oz frozen
   spinach, thawed

4 tbsp chopped fresh
   flat-leaf parsley

2 tbsp chopped fresh dill

3 eggs, beaten

200 g/7 oz feta cheese

salt and pepper

100 g/3$\frac{1}{2}$ oz butter

225 g/8 oz filo pastry (work
   with one sheet at a time
   and keep the remaining
   sheets covered with a
   damp tea towel)

method

1 To make the filling, heat the oil in a saucepan, then add the onion and fry until softened. Add the fresh spinach if using, with only the water clinging to the leaves after washing, or the frozen spinach, and cook for 2–5 minutes, until just wilted. Remove from the heat and set aside to cool.

2 When the mixture has cooled, add the parsley, dill and eggs. Crumble in the cheese, season with salt and pepper and mix well.

3 Melt the butter and use a little to grease a deep 30 x 20-cm/12 x 8-inch metal baking tin. Cut the pastry sheets in half widthways. Take 1 sheet of pastry and use it to line the base and sides of the tin. Brush the pastry with a little of the melted butter. Repeat until half of the pastry sheets are used, brushing each one with butter.

4 Spread the filling over the pastry, then top with the remaining pastry sheets, brushing each with butter and tucking down the edges. Using a sharp knife, score the top layers of the pastry into 6 squares.

5 Bake in a preheated oven, 190°C/375°F/Gas Mark 5, for about 40 minutes, until golden brown. Serve hot or cold.

spanish tortilla

ingredients

MAKES 8–10 SLICES

125 ml/4 fl oz olive oil
600 g/1 lb 5 oz potatoes,
    peeled and thinly sliced
1 large onion, thinly sliced
6 large eggs
salt and pepper
fresh flat-leaf parsley sprigs,
    to garnish

method

1 Heat a 25-cm/10-inch frying pan over a high heat. Add the oil and heat. Reduce the heat, then add the potatoes and onion and cook for 15–20 minutes, until the potatoes are tender.

2 Beat the eggs in a large bowl and season generously. Drain the potatoes and onion through a sieve over a heatproof bowl to reserve the oil. Very gently stir the vegetables into the eggs. Let stand for 10 minutes.

3 Wipe out the frying pan, add 4 tablespoons of the reserved oil, and heat over a medium–high heat. Add the egg mixture and press the potatoes and onions into an even layer.

4 Cook for about 5 minutes, shaking the frying pan occasionally, until the bottom is set. Use a spatula to loosen the side of the tortilla. Place a large plate over the top and carefully invert the frying pan and plate together so the tortilla drops onto the plate.

5 Add 1 tablespoon of the remaining reserved oil to the frying pan and swirl around. Carefully slide the tortilla back into the frying pan, cooked side up. Run the spatula round the tortilla and continue cooking for 3 minutes, or until the eggs are set and the bottom is golden brown. Remove from the heat and slide the tortilla onto a plate. Let stand for at least 5 minutes before cutting. Garnish with parsley sprigs and serve warm or at room temperature.

roasted pepper salad

ingredients

SERVES 8

3 red peppers

3 yellow peppers

5 tbsp Spanish extra virgin
   olive oil

2 tbsp dry sherry vinegar or
   lemon juice

2 garlic cloves, crushed

pinch of sugar

salt and pepper

1 tbsp capers

8 small black Spanish olives

2 tbsp chopped fresh
   marjoram, plus extra
   sprigs to garnish

method

1 Place the peppers on a wire rack or grill pan and cook under a grill preheated to high for 10 minutes, turning them frequently, until their skins have blackened and blistered.

2 Remove the roasted peppers from the heat, and either put them in a bowl and immediately cover tightly with a clean, damp tea towel, or put them in a plastic bag. The steam helps to soften the skins and makes it easier to remove them. Let the peppers stand for about 15 minutes, until they are cool enough to handle.

3 Holding one pepper at a time over a clean bowl, use a sharp knife to make a small hole in the base and gently squeeze out the juices and reserve them. Still holding the pepper over the bowl, carefully peel off the blackened skin with your fingers or a knife and discard it. Cut the peppers in half and remove the stem, core and seeds, then cut each pepper into neat thin strips. Arrange the pepper strips on a serving dish.

4 To the reserved pepper juices add the olive oil, sherry vinegar, garlic, sugar, salt and pepper. Whisk together until combined. Drizzle the dressing evenly over the salad.

5 Sprinkle the capers, olives and chopped marjoram over the salad, garnish with marjoram sprigs and serve at room temperature.

greek salad

ingredients

SERVES 4

4 tomatoes, cut into wedges

1 onion, sliced

$^1/_2$ cucumber, sliced

225 g/8 oz kalamata olives,
    stoned

225 g/8 oz feta cheese,
    cubed (drained weight)

2 tbsp fresh coriander leaves

fresh flat-leaf parsley,
    to garnish

pitta bread, to serve

dressing

5 tbsp extra virgin olive oil

2 tbsp white wine vinegar

1 tbsp lemon juice

$^1/_2$ tsp sugar

1 tbsp chopped fresh
    coriander

salt and pepper

method

1 To make the dressing, place the oil, vinegar, lemon juice, sugar and coriander in a large bowl. Season with salt and pepper and mix together well.

2 Add the tomatoes, onion, cucumber, olives, feta cheese and coriander. Toss all the ingredients together, then divide between four individual serving bowls. Garnish with fresh parsley and serve with pitta bread.

tabbouleh

ingredients

SERVES 4

175 g/6 oz bulgar wheat

3 tbsp extra virgin olive oil

4 tbsp lemon juice

salt and pepper

4 spring onions

1 green pepper,
    deseeded and sliced

4 tomatoes, chopped

2 tbsp chopped
    fresh parsley

2 tbsp chopped fresh mint

8 black olives, stoned

chopped fresh mint, to
    garnish

method

1 Place the bulgar wheat in a large bowl and add enough cold water to cover. Let stand for 30 minutes, or until the wheat has doubled in size. Drain well and press out as much liquid as possible. Spread out the wheat on kitchen paper to dry.

2 Place the wheat in a serving bowl. Mix the olive oil and lemon juice together in a jug and season with salt and pepper. Pour the lemon mixture over the wheat and marinate for 1 hour.

3 Using a sharp knife, finely chop the spring onions, then add to the salad with the green pepper, tomatoes, parsley and mint and toss lightly to mix. Top the salad with the olives and garnish with the chopped mint, then serve immediately.

baking
& desserts

The secret of the success of the Mediterranean diet, and its contribution towards a long and healthy life, is perhaps partly a question of balance. Alongside all the fantastic ingredients that combine to promote a healthy heart, there is still room for more than a little indulgence!

Bread is baked fresh daily and eaten with every meal – Olive & Sun-dried Tomato Bread and Mini Focaccia make an excellent accompaniment to everything from a simple grilled fish dish to a rich, meaty stew, while Walnut Cheese Wafers make a protein-packed partner to salads.

And for that sweet tooth? There's plenty to satisfy it here! Mediterranean cakes and desserts make wonderful use of regional ingredients, such as nuts and citrus fruits – try Moroccan Orange & Almond Cake, Almond Tart or Lemon Tart. Ice creams and chilled desserts are a refreshing foil to the summer sun – Pistachio Ice Cream, Sicilian Ice Cream Cake and Lemon Sorbet with Cava are all lovely, and the Frozen Almond Cream with Hot Chocolate Sauce is divine.

If that healthy heart is your main concern, the Baked Apricots with Honey and Grilled Honey Figs with Zabaglione are a Mediterranean treat for you.

olive & sun-dried tomato bread

ingredients

SERVES 4

400 g/14 oz plain flour, plus extra for dusting

1 tsp salt

1 sachet easy-blend dried yeast

1 tsp brown sugar

1 tbsp chopped fresh thyme

200 ml/7 fl oz warm water (heated to 50°C/122°F)

4 tbsp olive oil, plus extra for oiling

50 g/1³/₄ oz black olives, stoned and sliced

50 g/1³/₄ oz green olives, stoned and sliced

100 g/3¹/₂ oz sun-dried tomatoes in oil, drained and sliced

1 egg yolk, beaten

method

1 Place the flour, salt and yeast in a bowl and mix together, then stir in the sugar and thyme. Make a well in the centre. Slowly stir in enough water and oil to make a dough. Mix in the olives and sun-dried tomatoes. Knead the dough for 5 minutes, then form it into a ball. Brush a bowl with oil, add the dough and cover with clingfilm. Let rise in a warm place for about 1¹/2 hours, or until it has doubled in size.

2 Dust a baking sheet with flour. Knead the dough lightly, then cut into two halves and shape into ovals or circles. Place them on the baking sheet, cover with clingfilm and let rise again in a warm place for 45 minutes, or until they have doubled in size.

3 Make 3 shallow diagonal cuts on the top of each piece of dough. Brush with the egg. Bake in a preheated oven, 200°C/400°F/ Gas Mark 6, for 40 minutes, or until cooked through – the loaves should be golden on top and sound hollow when tapped on the bottom. Transfer to wire racks to cool.

mini focaccia

ingredients

SERVES 4

350 g/12 oz strong white
   flour, plus extra for dusting
$^1/_2$ tsp salt
7-g/$^1/_4$-oz sachet easy-blend
   dried yeast
2 tbsp olive oil, plus extra
   for oiling
250 ml/8 fl oz lukewarm water
100 g/3$^1/_2$ oz stoned green or
   black olives, halved

topping

2 red onions, sliced
2 tbsp olive oil
1 tsp sea salt
1 tbsp thyme leaves

method

1 Sift the flour and salt into a large bowl. Stir in the yeast, pour in the oil and water and mix to form a dough. Turn the dough out onto a floured work surface and knead for 5 minutes. Alternatively, use an electric mixer with a dough hook.

2 Place the dough in an oiled bowl, cover and let stand in a warm place for 1–1$^1/_2$ hours, or until doubled in size. Punch down the dough by kneading it again for 1–2 minutes.

3 Knead half of the olives into the dough. Divide the dough into quarters and shape the quarters into circles. Place them on an oiled baking sheet and push your fingers into the dough to create a dimpled effect.

4 To make the topping, sprinkle the red onions and remaining olives over the circles. Drizzle the oil over the top and sprinkle with the sea salt and thyme leaves. Cover and let stand for 30 minutes.

5 Bake in a preheated oven, 190°C/375°F/ Gas Mark 5, for 20–25 minutes, or until the focaccia are golden. Transfer to a wire rack to cool before serving.

walnut cheese wafers

ingredients

MAKES ABOUT 38

40 g/1 1/2 oz walnut pieces

115 g/4 oz plain flour, plus
   extra for dusting

salt and pepper

115 g/4 oz butter

115 g/4 oz feta cheese

beaten egg, for glazing

method

1 Put the walnuts in a food processor and chop finely. Remove from the processor and set aside.

2 Add the flour, salt and pepper to the processor bowl. Cut the butter into small pieces, add to the flour and mix, in short bursts, until the mixture resembles fine breadcrumbs. Roughly grate in the cheese, add the reserved walnuts and mix quickly to form a dough.

3 Turn the mixture onto a lightly floured work surface and roll out thinly. Using a 6-cm/ 2 1/4-inch round biscuit cutter, cut the dough into rounds and place on baking sheets. Brush the tops with beaten egg.

4 Bake the wafers in a preheated oven, 190°C/ 375°F/Gas Mark 5, for about 10 minutes, until golden. Cool on a wire rack.

5 Store in an airtight tin.

almond biscuits

ingredients

MAKES ABOUT 60

150 g/5^1/$_2$ oz butter, at room
temperature, plus extra for
greasing
150 g/5^1/$_2$ oz caster sugar
115 g/4 oz plain flour
25 g/1 oz ground almonds
pinch of salt
75 g/2^3/$_4$ oz blanched
almonds, lightly toasted
and finely chopped
finely grated rind of
1 large lemon
4 medium egg whites

method

1 Put the butter and sugar into a bowl and beat until light and fluffy. Sift over the flour, ground almonds and salt, tipping in any ground almonds left in the sieve. Use a large metal spoon to fold in the chopped almonds and lemon rind.

2 In a separate, spotlessly clean bowl, whisk the egg whites until soft peaks form. Fold the egg whites into the almond mixture.

3 Drop small teaspoonfuls of the mixture onto one or more well-greased baking sheets, spacing them well apart (you might need to cook in batches). Bake in a preheated oven, 180°C/350°F/Gas Mark 4, for 15–20 minutes until the biscuits are golden brown at the edges. Transfer to a wire rack to cool completely. Continue baking until all the mixture is used. Store in an airtight container for up to 1 week.

baklava

ingredients

SERVES 4

150 g/5¹/2 oz shelled
    pistachio nuts, finely
    chopped
75 g/2³/4 oz toasted
    hazelnuts, finely chopped
75 g/2³/4 oz blanched
    hazelnuts, finely chopped
grated rind of 1 lemon
1 tbsp brown sugar
1 tsp ground mixed spice
150 g/5¹/2 oz butter, melted,
    plus extra for greasing
250 g/9 oz (about 16 sheets)
    frozen filo pastry, thawed
250 ml/8 fl oz water
2 tbsp clear honey
1 tbsp lemon juice
300 g/10¹/2 oz caster sugar
¹/2 tsp ground cinnamon

method

1 Place the nuts, lemon rind, brown sugar and mixed spice in a bowl and mix well. Grease a round cake tin, 18 cm/7 inches in diameter and 5 cm/2 inches deep, with butter. Cut the whole stack of filo sheets to the size of the tin, then keep the rounds covered with a damp tea towel.

2 Lay one round on the base of the pan and brush with melted butter. Add another 6 rounds on top, brushing between each layer with melted butter. Spread over one-third of the nut mixture, then add 3 rounds of buttered filo. Spread over another third of the nut mixture then top with 3 more rounds of buttered filo. Spread over the remaining nut mixture and add the last 3 rounds of buttered filo. Cut into wedges, then bake in a preheated oven, 160°C/325°F/Gas Mark 3, for 1 hour.

3 Meanwhile, place the water, honey, lemon juice, caster sugar and cinnamon in a saucepan. Bring to the boil, stirring. Reduce the heat and simmer, without stirring, for 15 minutes, then remove from the heat and cool. Remove the baklava from the oven, pour over the syrup and allow to set before serving.

moroccan orange & almond cake

ingredients

**MAKES 1 X
20-CM/8-INCH CAKE**

1 orange

115 g/4 oz butter, softened,
    plus extra for greasing

115 g/4 oz golden caster
    sugar

2 eggs, beaten

175 g/6 oz semolina

100 g/3½ oz ground almonds

1½ tsp baking powder

icing sugar, for dusting

Greek-style yogurt, to serve

syrup

300 ml/10 fl oz orange juice

130 g/4¾ oz caster sugar

8 cardamom pods, crushed

method

1 Grate the rind from the orange, reserving some for the decoration, and squeeze the juice from one half. Place the butter, orange rind and caster sugar in a bowl and beat together until light and fluffy. Gradually beat in the eggs.

2 In a separate bowl, mix the semolina, ground almonds and baking powder, then fold into the creamed mixture with the orange juice. Spoon the batter into a greased and base-lined 20-cm/ 8-inch cake tin and bake in a preheated oven, 180°C/350°F/Gas Mark 4, for 30–40 minutes, until well risen and a skewer inserted into the centre comes out clean. Cool the cake in the tin for 10 minutes.

3 To make the syrup, place the orange juice, sugar and cardamom pods in a saucepan over a low heat and stir until the sugar has dissolved. Bring to the boil and simmer for 4 minutes, or until syrupy.

4 Turn the cake out into a deep serving dish. Using a skewer, make holes all over the surface of the warm cake. Strain the syrup into a separate bowl and spoon three quarters of it over the cake, then let stand for 30 minutes. Dust with icing sugar and serve with the remaining syrup drizzled around and Greek-style yogurt decorated with the reserved orange rind.

almond tart

ingredients

**MAKES 1 X
25-CM/10-INCH TART**

pastry

280 g/10 oz plain flour

150 g/5^1/2 oz caster sugar

1 tsp finely grated lemon rind

pinch of salt

150 g/5^1/2 oz unsalted butter,
    chilled and cut into
    small dice, plus extra
    for greasing

1 medium egg, lightly beaten

1 tbsp chilled water

filling

175 g/6 oz unsalted butter,
    at room temperature

175 g/6 oz caster sugar

3 large eggs

175 g/6 oz finely
    ground almonds

2 tsp plain flour

1 tbsp finely grated orange rind

^{1}/2 tsp almond essence

icing sugar, to decorate

soured cream (optional), to
    serve

method

1 To make the pastry, put the flour, sugar, lemon rind and salt in a bowl. Rub or cut in the butter until the mixture resembles fine breadcrumbs. Combine the egg and water, then slowly pour into the flour, stirring with a fork until a coarse mass forms. Shape into a ball and chill for at least 1 hour.

2 Roll out the pastry on a lightly floured work surface until 3 mm/^{1}/8 inch thick. Use to line a greased 25-cm/10-inch tart pan. Return to the refrigerator for at least 15 minutes, then cover the pastry case with foil and fill with baking beans. Place in a preheated oven, 220°C/425°F/Gas Mark 7, and bake for 12 minutes. Remove the baking beans and foil and return the pastry case to the oven for 4 minutes to dry the base. Remove from the oven and reduce the oven temperature to 200°C/400°F/Gas Mark 6.

3 Meanwhile, make the filling. Beat the butter and sugar until creamy. Beat in the eggs, one at a time. Add the almonds, flour, orange rind and almond essence, and beat until blended.

4 Spoon the filling into the pastry case and smooth the surface. Bake for 30–35 minutes until the top is golden and the tip of a knife inserted in the centre comes out clean. Cool completely on a wire rack, then dust with sifted icing sugar. Serve with soured cream, if liked.

lemon tart

ingredients

SERVES 8

300 g/10 oz ready-made
    sweet pastry
finely grated rind of 3 lemons
150 ml/5 fl oz freshly
    squeezed lemon juice
    from 3 or 4 large lemons
100 g/3^1/$_2$ oz caster sugar
150 ml/5 fl oz soured cream
3 large eggs, plus
    3 large egg yolks
icing sugar, for dusting

method

1 Roll out the pastry and use to line a 23-cm/ 9-inch fluted tart tin with a removable base, leaving the excess pastry hanging over the edge. Line the pastry case with a larger piece of waxed paper, then fill with baking beans.

2 Put the lined tart tin on a preheated baking sheet and bake in a preheated oven, 200°C/ 400°F/Gas Mark 6, for 10–15 minutes, or until the pastry rim looks set. Remove the paper and beans and return the pastry case to the oven for a further 5 minutes, or until the bottom looks dry. Remove the pastry case from the oven, then leave it on the baking sheet and reduce the oven temperature to 190°C/375°F/Gas Mark 5.

3 Meanwhile, beat the lemon rind, lemon juice and caster sugar together until the sugar dissolves. Slowly beat in the soured cream until blended, then beat in the eggs and yolks, one at a time.

4 Carefully pour the filling into the pastry case, then transfer to the oven and bake for 20–30 minutes, or until the filling is set and the pastry is golden brown. If the pastry, or the filling, looks as though it is becoming too brown, cover the tart with a sheet of foil.

5 Transfer the tart to a cooling rack, then roll a rolling pin over the edge to remove the excess pastry. To serve, remove the tin and transfer to a serving plate. Dust with icing sugar.

espresso crème brûlée

ingredients

SERVES 4

450 ml/16 fl oz double cream

1 tbsp instant espresso
  powder

4 large egg yolks

100 g/3¹/₂ oz caster sugar

2 tbsp coffee liqueur

4 tbsp caster sugar,
  for glazing

method

1 Place the cream in a small saucepan over a medium–high heat and heat until small bubbles appear around the edges. Mix in the espresso powder, stirring until it dissolves, then remove the pan from the heat and cool completely.

2 Lightly beat the egg yolks in a bowl, then add the sugar and continue beating until thick and creamy. Reheat the cream over a medium–high heat until small bubbles appear around the edges. Stir into the egg-yolk mixture, beating constantly. Stir in the coffee liqueur.

3 Divide the custard mixture between 4 shallow white porcelain dishes placed on a baking sheet. Bake the custards in a preheated oven, 110°C/225°F/Gas Mark ¹/₄, for 35–40 minutes, or until the custard is just 'trembling' when you shake the dishes.

4 Remove the custards from the oven and cool completely. Cover the surfaces with clingfilm and chill in the refrigerator for at least 4 hours, but ideally overnight.

5 Just before you are ready to serve, sprinkle the surface of each custard with the remaining sugar and caramelize with a kitchen blow-torch, or put the dishes under a very hot preheated grill, until the topping is golden and bubbling. Cool for a few minutes for the caramel to harden before serving.

spanish caramel custard

ingredients

SERVES 6

500 ml/18 fl oz whole milk

1/2 orange with 2 long, thin pieces of rind removed and reserved

1 vanilla pod, split, or 1/2 tsp vanilla essence

175 g/6 oz caster sugar

butter, for greasing

3 large eggs, plus 2 large egg yolks

method

1 Pour the milk into a saucepan with the orange rind and vanilla pod. Bring to the boil, then remove from the heat and stir in 85 g/3 oz of the sugar; set aside for at least 30 minutes to infuse.

2 Meanwhile, put the remaining sugar and 4 tablespoons of water in another saucepan over a medium–high heat. Stir until the sugar dissolves, then boil without stirring until the caramel turns deep golden brown. Immediately remove from the heat and squeeze in a few drops of orange juice to stop the cooking. Pour into a lightly buttered 1.2-litre/2-pint soufflé dish and swirl to cover the base; set aside.

3 Return the pan of infused milk to the heat, and bring to a simmer. Beat the whole eggs and egg yolks together in a heatproof bowl. Pour the warm milk into the eggs, whisking constantly. Strain into the soufflé dish.

4 Place the soufflé dish in a roasting tin and pour enough boiling water into the tin to come halfway up the sides of the dish. Bake in a preheated oven, 160°C/325°F/Gas Mark 3, for 75–90 minutes until set and a knife inserted in the centre comes out clean. Remove the soufflé dish from the roasting tin and set aside to cool completely. Cover and chill overnight. To serve, run a metal spatula round the soufflé, then invert onto a serving plate, shaking firmly to release.

pistachio ice cream

ingredients

SERVES 4

300 ml/10 fl oz double cream

150 g/5^1/$_2$ oz Greek-style yogurt

2 tbsp milk

3 tbsp Greek honey

green food colouring

50 g/1^3/$_4$ oz shelled unsalted pistachio nuts, finely chopped

pistachio praline

oil, for brushing

150 g/5^1/$_2$ oz granulated sugar

3 tbsp water

50 g/1^3/$_4$ oz shelled, whole, unsalted pistachio nuts

method

1 Set the freezer to its coldest setting. Put the cream, yogurt, milk and honey in a bowl and mix together. Add a few drops of green food colouring to tint the mixture pale green and stir in well. Pour the mixture into a shallow freezer container and freeze, uncovered, for 1–2 hours, until beginning to set around the edges. Turn the mixture into a bowl and, with a fork, stir until smooth, then stir in the pistachio nuts. Return to the freezer container, cover and freeze for another 2–3 hours, until firm. Alternatively, use an ice cream maker, following the manufacturer's instructions.

2 To make the pistachio praline, brush a baking sheet with oil. Put the sugar and water in a saucepan and heat gently, stirring, until the sugar has dissolved, then let bubble gently, without stirring, for 6–10 minutes, until lightly golden brown.

3 Remove the pan from the heat and stir in the pistachio nuts. Immediately pour the mixture onto the baking sheet and spread out evenly. Stand it in a cool place for about 1 hour, until cold and hardened, then put it in a plastic bag and crush with a hammer.

4 About 30 minutes before serving, remove the ice cream from the freezer and stand it at room temperature to soften slightly. To serve, scatter the praline over the ice cream.

sicilian ice cream cake

ingredients

SERVES 4

Genoa sponge cake

6 eggs, separated

200 g/7 oz caster sugar

85 g/3 oz self-raising flour

85 g/3 oz cornflour

filling

500 g/1 lb 2 oz ricotta cheese

200 g/7 oz caster sugar

600 ml/1 pint Maraschino
    liqueur

85 g/3 oz unsweetened
    chocolate, chopped

200 g/7 oz mixed candied
    peel, diced

300 ml/10 fl oz double cream

candied cherries, angelica
    and citrus fruit, and
    flaked almonds, to
    decorate

method

1 Beat the egg yolks with the sugar until pale and frothy. In a separate, spotlessly clean bowl, whisk the whites until stiff peaks form. Gently fold the whites into the egg yolk mixture with a figure-of-eight action.

2 Sift the flour and cornflour into a bowl, then sift into the egg mixture and gently fold in. Pour the mixture into a 25-cm/10-inch cake tin lined with parchment paper, and level the surface. Bake in a preheated oven, 180°C/ 350°F/Gas Mark 4, for 30 minutes, until springy to the touch. Turn out onto a wire rack, remove the lining paper and cool completely.

3 For the filling, combine the ricotta, sugar and 425 ml/15 fl oz of the Maraschino in a bowl, beating well. Stir in the chopped chocolate and the candied peel.

4 Cut the sponge cake into strips about 1 cm/ 1/2 inch wide and use some of it to line the bottom and sides of a 900-g/2-lb loaf tin. Set aside the remaining slices.

5 Spoon the ricotta mixture into the tin and level the surface. Cover with the reserved sponge cake. Drizzle the remaining Maraschino over the top, then chill overnight. To serve, turn out onto a serving plate. Whisk the cream until stiff and coat the top and sides of the cake. Decorate with the candied cherries, angelica and citrus fruit, and the almonds.

lemon sorbet with cava

ingredients

SERVES 4–6

3–4 lemons

250 ml/9 fl oz water

200 g/7 oz caster sugar

1 bottle Spanish cava, chilled,
    to serve

method

1 Roll the lemons on the work surface, pressing firmly, which helps to release the juice. Pare off a few strips of rind and set aside for decoration, then finely grate the rind from 3 lemons. Squeeze the juice from as many of the lemons as is necessary to give 175 ml/6 fl oz.

2 Put the water and sugar in a heavy-based saucepan over a medium–high heat and stir to dissolve the sugar. Bring to the boil, without stirring, and boil for 2 minutes. Remove from the heat, stir in the lemon rind, cover and stand for 30 minutes, or until cool.

3 When the mixture is cool, stir in the lemon juice. Strain into an ice cream maker and freeze according to the manufacturer's instructions. (Alternatively, strain the mixture into a freezerproof container and freeze for 2 hours, or until mushy and freezing round the edges. Tip into a bowl, beat and return to the freezer. Repeat the process twice more.) Ten minutes before serving, remove the sorbet from the freezer, to soften.

4 To serve, scoop into 4–6 tall glasses, decorate with the reserved rind, if using, and top up with cava.

frozen almond cream with hot chocolate sauce

ingredients

SERVES 4–6

175 g/6 oz blanched almonds

300 ml/10 fl oz double cream

1/4 tsp almond essence

150 ml/5 fl oz single cream

55 g/2 oz icing sugar

hot chocolate sauce

100 g/3 1/2 oz plain chocolate, broken into pieces

3 tbsp golden syrup

4 tbsp water

25 g/1 oz unsalted butter, diced

1/4 tsp vanilla essence

method

1 Toast the almonds on a baking sheet in a preheated oven, 200°C/400°F/Gas Mark 6, for 7–10 minutes, stirring occasionally, until golden brown. Immediately tip onto a cutting board to cool. Roughly chop half the nuts and finely grind the remainder.

2 Whip the double cream with the almond essence until soft peaks form. Stir in the single cream and continue whipping, sifting in the sugar in 3 batches. Transfer to an ice cream maker and freeze. When the cream is almost frozen, transfer it to a bowl, and stir in the chopped almonds. Put the mixture in a 450-g/ 1-lb loaf tin and smooth the top. Wrap in foil and put in the freezer for at least 3 hours.

3 To make the hot chocolate sauce, place a heatproof bowl over a saucepan of simmering water. Add the chocolate, syrup and water and stir until the chocolate melts. Stir in the butter and vanilla essence until smooth.

4 To serve, dip the bottom of the loaf tin in boiling water for a couple of seconds. Invert onto a cutting board, giving a sharp shake to release the frozen cream. Coat the top and sides with the finely chopped almonds. Use a warm knife to slice into 8–12 slices. Arrange two slices on each plate and spoon over the hot chocolate sauce.

mascarpone creams

ingredients

SERVES 4

115 g/4 oz amaretti biscuits,
    crushed

4 tbsp amaretto or
    maraschino

4 eggs, separated

55 g/2 oz caster sugar

225 g/8 oz mascarpone
    cheese

toasted flaked almonds,
    to decorate

method

1 Place the amaretti crumbs in a bowl, add the amaretto or maraschino, and set aside to soak.

2 Meanwhile, beat the egg yolks with the caster sugar until pale and thick. Fold in the mascarpone and soaked biscuit crumbs.

3 Whisk the egg white in a separate, spotlessly clean bowl until stiff, then gently fold into the cheese mixture. Divide the mascarpone cream between 4 serving dishes and chill for 1–2 hours. Sprinkle with toasted flaked almonds just before serving.

chocolate & cherry tiramisù

ingredients

SERVES 4

200 ml/7 fl oz strong black
  coffee, cooled to room
  temperature
6 tbsp cherry brandy
16 trifle sponges
250 g/9 oz mascarpone
300 ml/10 fl oz double cream,
  lightly whipped
3 tbsp icing sugar
275 g/9¾ oz sweet cherries,
  halved and stoned
60 g/2¼ oz chocolate curls or
  grated chocolate
whole cherries, to decorate

method

1 Pour the cooled coffee into a jug and stir in the cherry brandy. Put half of the trifle sponges into the bottom of a serving dish, then pour over half of the coffee mixture.

2 Put the mascarpone into a separate bowl along with the cream and sugar, and mix well. Spread half of the mascarpone mixture over the coffee-soaked trifle sponges, then top with half of the cherries. Arrange the remaining trifle sponges on top. Pour over the remaining coffee mixture and top with the remaining cherries. Finish with a layer of mascarpone mixture. Scatter over the chocolate curls, cover with clingfilm and chill in the refrigerator for at least 2 hours.

3 Remove from the refrigerator, decorate with whole cherries and serve.

grilled honey figs with zabaglione

ingredients

SERVES 4

8 fresh figs, cut in half

4 tbsp honey

2 fresh rosemary sprigs,
   leaves removed and finely
   chopped (optional)

3 eggs

method

1 Preheat the grill to high. Arrange the figs, cut-side up, on the grill pan. Brush with half the honey and sprinkle over the rosemary, if using.

2 Cook under the preheated grill for 5–6 minutes, or until just starting to caramelize.

3 Meanwhile, to make the zabaglione, lightly whisk the eggs with the remaining honey in a large, heatproof bowl, then place over a saucepan of simmering water. Using a hand-held electric whisk, beat the eggs and honey for 10 minutes, or until pale and thick.

4 Put 4 fig halves on each of 4 serving plates, add a generous spoonful of the zabaglione and serve immediately.

baked apricots with honey

ingredients

SERVES 4

butter, for greasing

4 apricots, each cut in half
and stoned

4 tbsp flaked almonds

4 tbsp honey

pinch ground ginger or grated
nutmeg

vanilla ice cream, to serve
(optional)

method

1 Lightly butter an ovenproof dish large enough to hold the apricot halves in a single layer.

2 Arrange the apricot halves in the dish, cut sides up. Sprinkle with the almonds and drizzle the honey over. Dust with the spice.

3 Bake in a preheated oven, 200°C/400°F/Gas Mark 6, for 12–15 minutes until the apricots are tender and the almonds golden. Remove from the oven and serve immediately, with ice cream on the side, if desired.

marsala cherries

ingredients

SERVES 4

140 g/5 oz caster sugar

thinly pared rind of 1 lemon

5-cm/2-inch piece of
    cinnamon stick

250 ml/8 fl oz water

250 ml/8 fl oz Marsala

900 g/2 lb morello cherries,
    stoned

150 ml/5 fl oz double cream

method

1 Put the sugar, lemon rind, cinnamon stick, water and Marsala in a heavy-based saucepan and bring to the boil, stirring constantly. Reduce the heat and simmer for 5 minutes. Remove the cinnamon stick.

2 Add the morello cherries, cover and simmer gently for 10 minutes. Using a slotted spoon, transfer the cherries to a bowl.

3 Return the pan to the heat and bring to the boil over a high heat. Boil for 3–4 minutes, until thick and syrupy. Pour the syrup over the cherries and set aside to cool, then chill for at least 1 hour.

4 Whisk the cream until stiff peaks form. Divide the cherries and syrup between 4 individual dishes or glasses, top with the cream and serve.